CLASSICAL
COMPOSERS

CLASSICAL
COMPOSERS

THE LIVES AND WORKS OF THE GREAT MUSICAL CREATORS OF THE
MEDIEVAL, BAROQUE AND CLASSICAL ERAS, WITH 200 ILLUSTRATIONS

WENDY THOMPSON

southwater

This edition is published by Southwater,
an imprint of Anness Publishing Ltd,
Hermes House, 88–89 Blackfriars Road, London SE1 8HA
tel. 020 7401 2077; fax 020 7633 9499

www.southwaterbooks.com; www.annesspublishing.com

Anness Publishing has a new picture agency outlet for images for publishing, promotions or advertising.
Please visit our website www.practicalpictures.com for more information.

UK distributor: Book Trade Services; tel. 0116 2759086; fax 0116 2759090;
uksales@booktradeservices.com; exportsales@booktradeservices.com
North American distributor: National Book Network; tel. 301 459 3366; fax 301 429 5746; www.nbnbooks.com
Australian distributor: Pan Macmillan Australia; tel. 1300 135 113; fax 1300 135 103; customer.service@macmillan.com.au
New Zealand distributor: David Bateman Ltd; tel. (09) 415 7664; fax (09) 415 8892

Publisher: Joanna Lorenz
Project Editor: Felicity Forster
Editor: Beverley Jollands

Designer: Michael Morey
Picture Researcher: Cathy Stastny
Production Controller: Claire Rae

Cover Picture Credits: AKG, London (front – *Instruments de musique* by Anne Vallayer-Coster; back – Bach, Mozart, Beethoven)

ETHICAL TRADING POLICY
Because of our ongoing ecological investment programme, you, as our customer, can have the pleasure and reassurance of
knowing that a tree is being cultivated on your behalf to naturally replace the materials used to make the book you are holding.
For further information about this scheme, go to www.annesspublishing.com/trees

Previously published as part of a larger volume, *The Great Composers*

PUBLISHER'S NOTE
Although the advice and information in this book are believed to be accurate and true at the time of going to press, neither the
authors nor the publisher can accept any legal responsibility or liability for any errors or omissions that may be made.

HALF TITLE PAGE: *Johann Sebastian Bach playing at the court of Frederick the Great in 1747.*
FRONTISPIECE: *An idealized artist's impression of Mozart conducting parts of his* Requiem *from his deathbed.*
TITLE PAGE: *Ludwig van Beethoven in later life, composing at the piano in his Viennese apartment.*

LEFT: *Detail of a boys' choir from the* Seven Joys of the Virgin Altarpiece *(c.1480) by the anonymous Master of the Holy Parent.*
OPPOSITE: *A musical party, painted by Per Hillestrom (1732–1816).*

Contents

Introduction

Music is the universal language of mankind.

Henry Wadsworth Longfellow (1807–82), "Outre-Mer"

Human beings have been making music for a very long time, although it was not until medieval times that systems were invented for writing it down. From the Middle Ages onwards, scholars have been able to study composition methods and styles, and how these developed over the centuries.

For the purposes of this book, the term "classical" is used in a broad sense, referring to the earliest written church music dating from the 12th century, through the 15th and 16th-century Renaissance, the Baroque era (c.1600–1750), and ending with the golden age of Western music in the Classical period (c.1750–1830). The book begins with a general history of classical composition, and is then divided into three sections covering the composers of the principal eras.

History of composition

The first section of the book traces how methods of composition have changed over time, from the earliest forms of notation in the 9th century AD through modes, keys, harmonization, Baroque forms, culminating in the Classical structure known as sonata form. The principal people and their methods involved in this transformation are highlighted along the way, for example Guido d'Arezzo's "solmization" system, Pythagoras's modes, Léonin and Pérotin's *ars antiqua* and *ars nova*, Handel's *opera seria*, Bach's Baroque suites, and Haydn's four-movement form and string quartet.

The book then charts the lives and times of the great classical composers, chronologically divided into the eras during which they lived.

The Middle Ages to the Renaissance

During the Middle Ages music was largely the preserve of the church, and the earliest music to survive was usually intended for sacred use. One of the earliest composers was Hildegard of Bingen, a 12th-century German abbess who wrote plainsong settings

ABOVE: Johann Sebastian Bach (1685–1750) is revered as one of the greatest of all composers. Some of his major works include the Brandenburg Concertos *(1721), the* Goldberg Variations *for harpsichord (1722),* St Matthew Passion *(1729) and* The Art of Fugue *(1750).*

of her own poetry. At around the same time, French composers Léonin and Pérotin were writing music for the Notre-Dame cathedral in Paris. Léonin was the first to indicate rhythm as well as pitch, and Pérotin created the first four-voice motets.

In the 14th century, polyphony (the simultaneous sounding of different notes) became increasingly prominent. The French composer Guillaume de Machaut was one of the first people to write music in four parts, when he set

ABOVE: Virginals were especially popular during Elizabethan times, particularly in domestic households. The Renaissance composer William Byrd (c.1543–1623) composed a great deal of virginals music – his pavans and galliards were much loved in the court of Queen Elizabeth I.

Instrumental forms, too, became increasingly popular during the Baroque era – particularly concertos, *concerti grossi*, sonatas and suites. Italian composers Arcangelo Corelli, Antonio Vivaldi and Domenico Scarlatti worked in these new forms, and Johann Sebastian Bach's *Brandenburg Concertos* and George Frideric Handel's set of *concerti grossi* brought the genre to its peak.

The Classical period

The period spanning c.1750–1830 corresponded to a period of classicism in art and architecture. The heavily ornate style of the Baroque era was replaced with a more restrained style, based on the classical proportions of the old world. Musical tastes emphasized clarity, order and balance, exemplified by the Classical symphony, the string quartet and the solo sonata.

The era was dominated by the First Viennese School: Joseph Haydn, Wolfgang Amadeus Mozart, Ludwig van Beethoven and Franz Schubert. Their works are still part of the core repertoire of classical music as a whole.

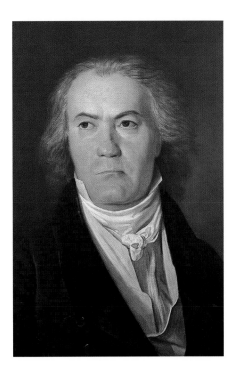

ABOVE: Ludwig van Beethoven (1770–1827) was renowned for his revolutionary artistic vision, shaped by the turbulent times in which he lived. His inner struggle is reflected in works such as the massive Eroica Symphony *(1803) and his opera* Fidelio *(1805). Despite the onset of total deafness by 1818, he completed his Symphony No. 9 (Choral, 1824) and several more piano sonatas and string quartets.*

ABOVE: As well as being the lead voice in the orchestra, the violin is an important solo instrument. Numerous composers have written concertos for the violin, for example Antonio Vivaldi (1678–1741), Johann Sebastian Bach (1685–1750) and Wolfgang Amadeus Mozart (1756–1791).

the Ordinary of the Mass to music. Polyphony went on to dominate Renaissance music, perfected by composers such as Giovanni Pierluigi da Palestrina, Orlande de Lassus, Tomás Luis de Victoria, Thomas Tallis and William Byrd.

The Baroque era

During the years from c.1600–1750 Renaissance polyphony gave way to a new, highly ornamental style with a strong harmonic basis. The Baroque era saw the introduction of many new forms, one of the most important being music-dramas, or opera. This new form flourished throughout Europe, transformed by composers such as Claudio Monteverdi, Antonio Vivaldi, Jean-Baptiste Lully, George Frideric Handel and Heinrich Schütz.

ABOVE: One of George Frideric Handel's (1685–1759) best-loved oratorio masterpieces, Messiah *(1742). This score shows a segment of the famous "Hallelujah chorus". This and many other of Handel's numerous oratorios are still regularly performed today.*

History
of
Composition

A beautiful example of a medieval choirbook emanating from Germany, now in the State Library in Gdańsk, Poland. The pages illustrated show the beginning of the plainsong chant for the antiphon Rorate coeli, *used in the liturgy for the Ascension season.*

Music as a Language

We – are we not formed, as notes of music are,
For one another, though dissimilar?

PERCY BYSSHE SHELLEY (1792–1822), "EPIPSYCHIDION"

Musical composition is one of the most mysterious of all art forms. People who can easily come to terms with a work of literature or a painting are still often baffled by the process by which a piece of music – appearing in material form as notation – must then be translated back into sound through the medium of a third party – the performer. Unlike a painting, a musical composition cannot be owned (except by its creator); and although a score may be published, like a book, it may remain incomprehensible to the general public until it is performed. Although a piece may be played thousands of times, each repetition is entirely individual, and interpretations by different players may vary widely.

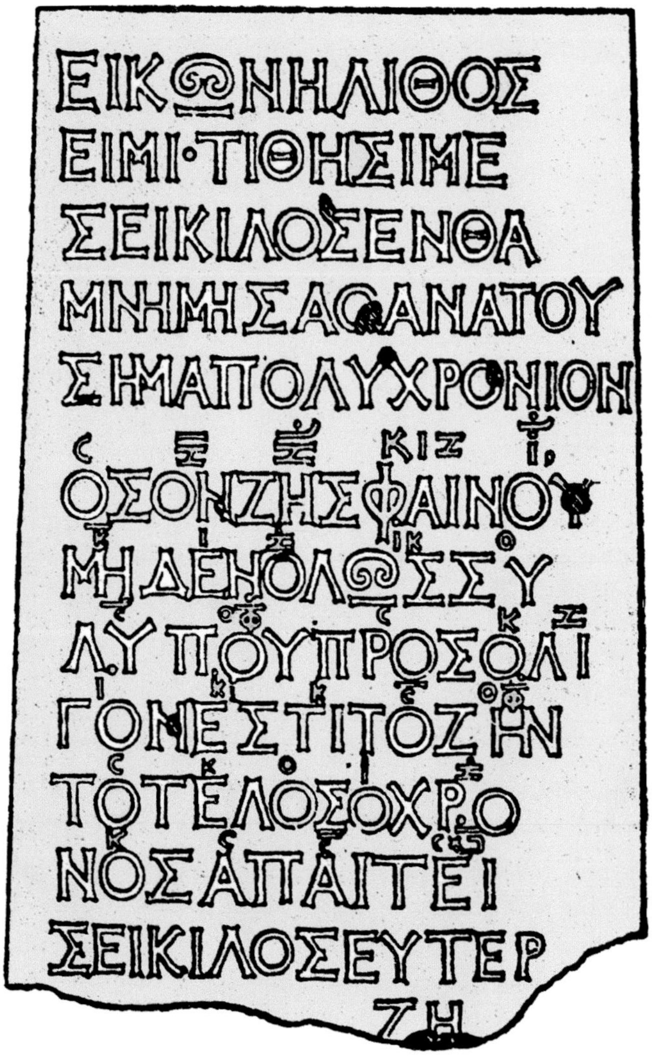

ABOVE: An early example of musical notation, a 3rd-century BC Greek song. The letters above the text indicate the notes.

Origins of musical notation

The earliest musical compositions were circumscribed by the range of the human voice. People from all cultures have always sung, or used primitive instruments to make sounds. Notation, or the writing down of music, developed to enable performers to remember what they had improvised, to preserve what they had created, and to facilitate interaction between more than one performer. Musical notation, like language, has ancient origins, dating back to the Middle East in the third millennium BC. The ancient Greeks appear to have been the first to try to represent variations of musical pitch through the medium of the alphabet, and successive civilizations all over the world attempted to formulate similar systems of recognizable musical notation.

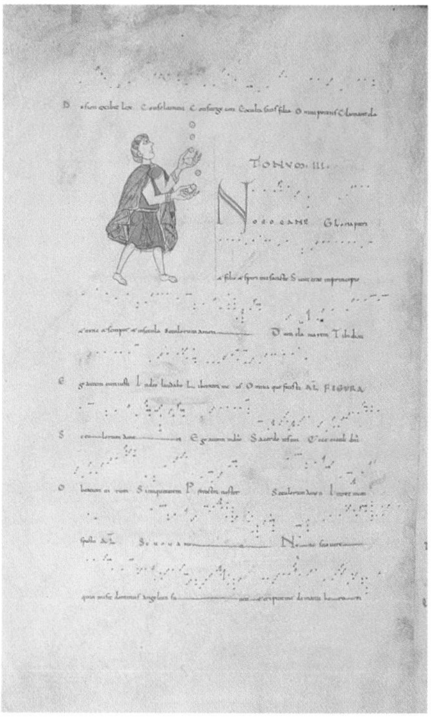

ABOVE: An early example of neumatic notation, from a German illustrated liturgical manuscript.

Neumatic notation

The earliest surviving Western European notational system was called "neumatic notation" – a system of symbols which attempted to portray the rise and fall of a melodic line. These date back to the 9th century AD, and were associated with the performance of sacred music – particularly plainsong – in monastic institutions. Several early manuscript

ABOVE: Guido d'Arezzo (c.977–1050), who devised the hexachord. His statue stands outside the Uffizi Gallery in Florence.

sources contain sacred texts with accompanying notation, although there was no standard system. The first appearance of staff notation, in which pitch was indicated by noteheads on or between lines with a symbol called a clef at the beginning to fix the pitch of one note, was in the 9th-century French treatise *Musica enchiriadis*. At the same time, music for instruments (particularly organ and lute) was beginning to be written down in diagrammatic form known as tablature, which indicated the positions of the player's fingers.

Guido d'Arezzo

The 11th-century Italian monk Guido d'Arezzo invented the "solmization" system – the precursor of "tonic solfa" – in which various syllables were used to indicate pitches in a musical scale. He also invented the "Guidonian Hand", in which the tips and joints of the five fingers

were used as an aid to remembering the various notes. At the same time, attempts were being made to indicate rhythm in performance, by varying the length and angle of the tails of the neumes, and the earliest polyphony (the simultaneous performance of more than one melodic line) was being explored.

The modal system

From around 400 BC until AD 1500, European music was built on modes. In the 4th century BC, the Greek mathematician Pythagoras worked out a scale roughly corresponding to the (modern-day) white keys of the piano, and two centuries later this scale was being used by the Greeks in seven different ways. The early Christian church adopted four so-called "authentic" modes (corresponding to white-note scales beginning on D, E, F and G), and under the 6th-century Pope Gregory, four more modes were added for the performance of plainsong.

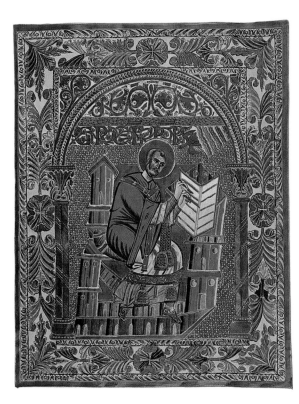

ABOVE: Pope Gregory (c.540–604), who gave his name to "Gregorian" plainsong melodies for liturgical use.

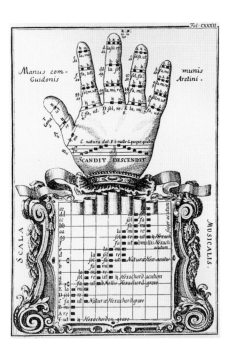

ABOVE: The so-called "Guidonian Hand", Guido d'Arezzo's device for showing the notes of the scale.

In 1547, the Swiss monk Henricus Glareanus postulated the theory of 12 modes, giving them somewhat inauthentic Greek names:

Dorian (range D–D)
HypoDorian (range A–A)
Phrygian (range E–E)
HypoPhrygian (range B–B)
Lydian (range F–F)
HypoLydian (range C–C)
Mixolydian (range G–G)
HypoMixolydian (range D–D)
Aeolian (range A–A)
HypoAeolian (range E–E)
Ionian (range C–C)
HypoIonian (range G–G)

Of these, the Aeolian and Ionian modes later became the basis of the minor and major scales respectively, which have since underpinned Western European music. The modes finally gave way to the keys we know today with the development of harmony in the late Renaissance period.

Emergence of Composers

Lovely forms do flow
From conceit divinely framed;
Heaven is music.

THOMAS CAMPION (1567–1620), "OBSERVATIONS IN THE ART OF ENGLISH POESIE"

Much medieval music survives in manuscript anthologies, some copied by monks for a particular monastery, others – often exquisitely illuminated – commissioned by an aristocratic patron. The earliest surviving ones date from the 10th century. Among the most famous manuscripts are two 15th-century English sources, the Old Hall Manuscript and the Eton College Choirbook. There are also two French sources dating from around 1470, the beautiful heart-shaped *Chansonnier cordiforme* and the *Mellon chansonnier*. Many pieces in these manuscripts are anonymous, but some were attributed to individual composers.

Ars antiqua

The Parisian composers Léonin and Pérotin were among the finest exponents of the style called *ars antiqua*, or "ancient style", a method of harmonizing plainsong melodies by adding between one and three secondary voices to the main vocal line, moving in parallel motion. This was known as *conductus*, and was an early form of polyphony – a compositional technique in which several melodic lines are combined, moving independently (as opposed to

ABOVE: *An example of the* ars antiqua *– a page from the* Jeu de Robin et Marion *by Adam de la Halle (1230–c.1288).*

homophony, in which the voices move together, forming blocks of harmony). European music was dominated by the polyphonic principle from the 13th to the 16th centuries.

By the 13th century, musical notation had become more sophisticated and standardized, with only the finer points of rhythmic

notation still open to interpretation. *Conductus* was gradually superseded by a new form known as the motet, a sacred Latin song, usually with a Biblical text, in which other voices moved in counterpoint to the main tune. The motet has remained a standard form of liturgical music.

Ars nova

At the same time, secular songs, such as those sung by French troubadours and *trouvères*, were being written down. Their flexibility and tunefulness led to the development of a new style (*ars nova*) in the 14th century, initiated by the theorist Philippe de Vitry. The music of the *ars nova*, which flourished particularly in France and Italy, had greater rhythmic vitality, and composers such as Guillaume de Machaut began to experiment with new techniques such as isorhythm, in which the same rhythmic pattern appears in successive repetitions of the melody, but not necessarily using notes of the same value. Many motets of the period were based on this technique, and on a *cantus firmus* – a familiar tune (either a plainsong melody or a folk song) which underpinned a polyphonic composition

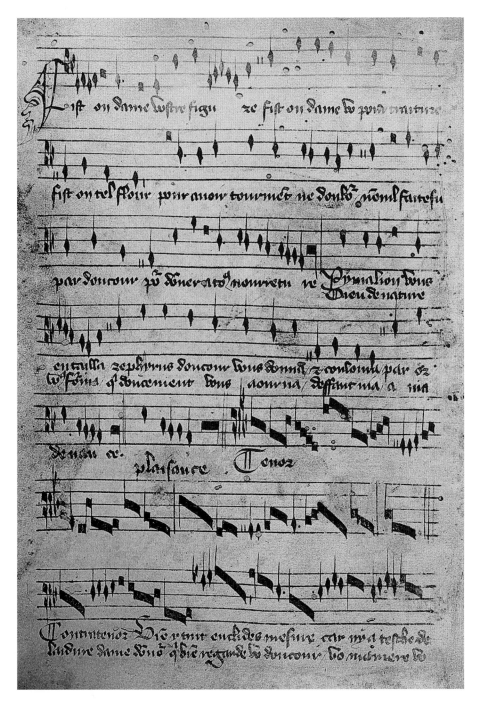

ABOVE: An example of ars nova *notation – an anonymous 14th-century French virelai (song). Note the increasing complexity of the notation.*

increasing sophistication of musical instruments. This was the invention of "monody", a new style in which the old principle of equal voices moving in counterpoint gave way to a single vocal line accompanied by instruments. While the tenor line still carried the main tune of a composition, it was now underpinned by a "ground bass", or *basso continuo* – a strong bass line played on keyboard and reinforced by cello and other bass instruments, which provided a harmonic foundation. The new style – the basis of all Baroque music – originated in Florence, where the composer Giulio Caccini published a famous collection of monodies, *Nuove musiche*, in 1602. The invention of monody coincided with the birth of a new secular musical genre, opera. The concept of a drama set to music, performed by costumed singers with instrumental accompaniment, originated in Florence with early examples by Peri and Caccini. Its greatest early exponent was Claudio Monteverdi.

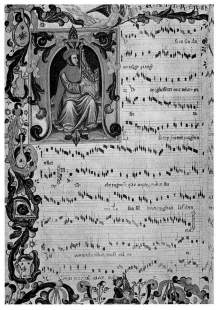

ABOVE: An exquisitely illuminated page from the 15th-century Squarcialupi codex *showing Francesco Landini (c.1325–97) with the score of his madrigal* Musica son.

by appearing throughout, usually in the tenor line.

By 1500 the system of Western European musical notation had become largely standardized, and from then onwards it became increasingly sophisticated and refined. The 16th century (the High Renaissance) was dominated by the principle of polyphony, brought to a height of perfection by composers such as Palestrina in Italy, Lassus in Germany, Victoria in Spain, and William Byrd in England.

Radical change of style

Around 1600, a musical sea-change occurred, partly as a reaction against polyphony, partly as a result of the secularization of society, and the

Baroque Forms

[Opera is] one of the most magnificent and expenseful diversions the wit of man can invent.

JOHN EVELYN (1620–1706), DIARY, 1645

Music in the Baroque era (c.1600–1750) was dominated by an insatiable demand for recreational art-forms. The great aristocratic and royal households, which could support their own orchestras, also employed composers to supply a constant need for new works. In 18th-century Europe, the growing size and wealth of the new middle classes led to a gradual democratization of musical appreciation and the advent of public performances in new concert halls and opera houses.

Music and drama

Opera became a favourite entertainment at the many princely courts which dotted Europe; the first public opera house opened in Venice in 1637, followed by others in major European cities. New musical forms were developed to suit the genre, including recitative and aria: the recitative allowed the singer (accompanied only by keyboard) to advance the story rapidly; while the aria, accompanied by the orchestra, allowed for expansive and lyrical reflection on a given situation or emotion.

The Baroque era was dominated by *opera seria*, based on plots drawn from ancient mythology, legend or history, with heroic characters fulfilling their destinies according to approved behavioural concepts. The most prolific 17th-century opera composers included

ABOVE: A sumptuous court entertainment of 1747 in the Teatro Argentina in Rome to celebrate the marriage of the son of Louis XV.

Alessandro Scarlatti and Antonio Vivaldi in Italy, Reinhard Keiser in Germany, and Jean-Baptiste Lully in France.

But by far the greatest exponent of Italian *opera seria* was Handel, who managed to make his characters express real human emotions. His operas have survived, while works by his contemporaries have been consigned to history. *Opera seria* lasted into Mozart's time, but by then audiences were demanding a lighter, more naturalistic type of drama, often dealing with comic subject-matter, which flowered in the hands of Gluck and especially Mozart.

Oratorio

Despite initial resistance, not even the church could remain unaffected by these new developments. A sacred – and normally unstaged – type of musical drama called oratorio, using the same musical forms as opera, but based on biblical stories, came into

being. Most opera composers (such as Scarlatti and Vivaldi) also wrote oratorios, but again it was Handel's fine examples which have survived to the present day. Bach's *St John* and *St Matthew Passions*, relating the story of Christ's death according to the Gospels, belong to this genre.

Instrumental forms

A growing demand for purely instrumental music led to the development of other new forms, such as the sonata. This was conceived both as a form suitable for church performance – the *sonata da chiesa*, which the Italian composer Corelli developed as a standard four-movement form – and its lighter counterpart the *sonata da camera*, which had an unspecified number of dance-like movements. Dance types – gavotte, minuet, courante, allemande, gigue – found their way into instrumental compositions, and their enormous variety formed the basis of the Baroque suite, perfected by Bach and Handel.

Another new form was the concerto, a genre pioneered by Giovanni Gabrieli in the late 1500s, in which a small group of instruments (later one solo instrument) is contrasted with the main body of the orchestra (the earlier form is known as a *concerto grosso*). While Renaissance music had exalted the principle of equality, Baroque music thrived on contrast.

Transition to Classicism

The still, sad music of humanity.

WILLIAM WORDSWORTH (1770–1850), "TINTERN ABBEY"

Baroque music reached its zenith in the works of Bach and Handel. Bach concentrated on sacred music, notably in his many cantatas – dramatic works for voices and instruments intended for church performance; Handel worked in both secular and sacred genres, writing Italian operas and English oratorios. The opening instrumental overtures, or "sinfonias", of such pieces gradually expanded into the 18th-century symphony, which eventually settled into a standard four-movement form with an opening fast movement, a lyrical slow movement, a short dance movement (usually a minuet and trio) and a fast finale. This was the form which Joseph Haydn perfected in over 100 examples, together with another new instrumental genre, the string quartet, written for two violins, viola and cello.

Sonata form

These works, together with the Classical sonata itself, were dominated by the structural principle of "sonata form", in which an opening exposition, usually presenting two main, contrasting themes, is succeeded by a central "development" section, in which the themes are subjected to a variety of treatments. Then comes

ABOVE: A group of musicians playing stringed and keyboard instruments at the court of the Duke of Modena in the late 17th century, painted by Antonio Gabbiani (1652–1726).

a "recapitulation", in which the opening themes are repeated (often in shortened or slightly varied form), followed by a short "coda" to round off the movement.

Haydn's great Viennese contemporaries Mozart and Beethoven consolidated and developed the symphony and string quartet, as well as the solo concerto – which was now becoming primarily a vehicle for one virtuoso performer. As the 18th-century harpsichord gave way to the more powerful and reliable pianoforte, the piano concerto – and the solo piano sonata – became favoured forms from Mozart's time onwards.

ABOVE: An 18th-century concert with wind, string and keyboard players held at a private Italian palazzo (probably in Venice).

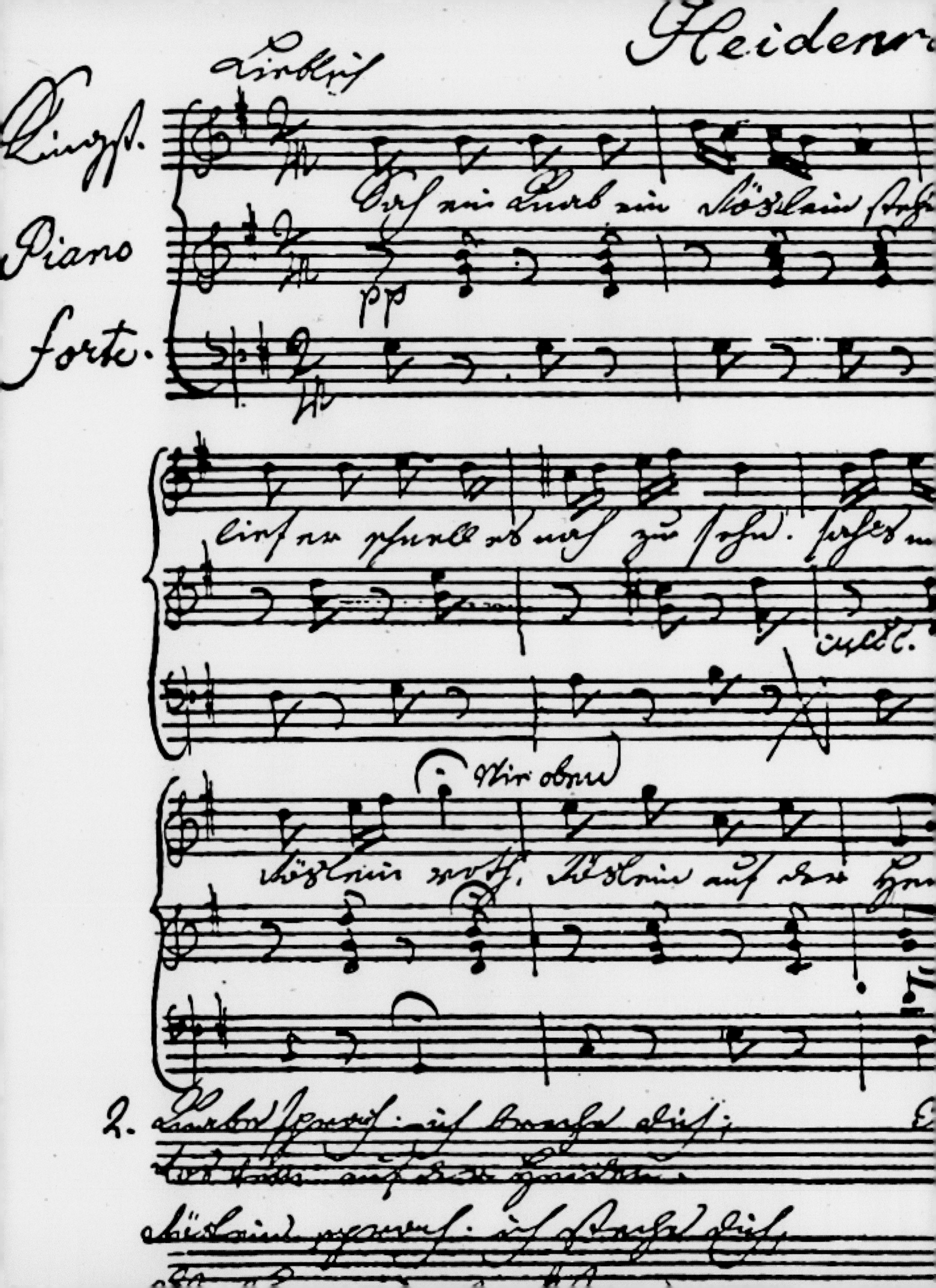
Heiden
Lieblich
Singst.
Piano
forte.
pp
2.

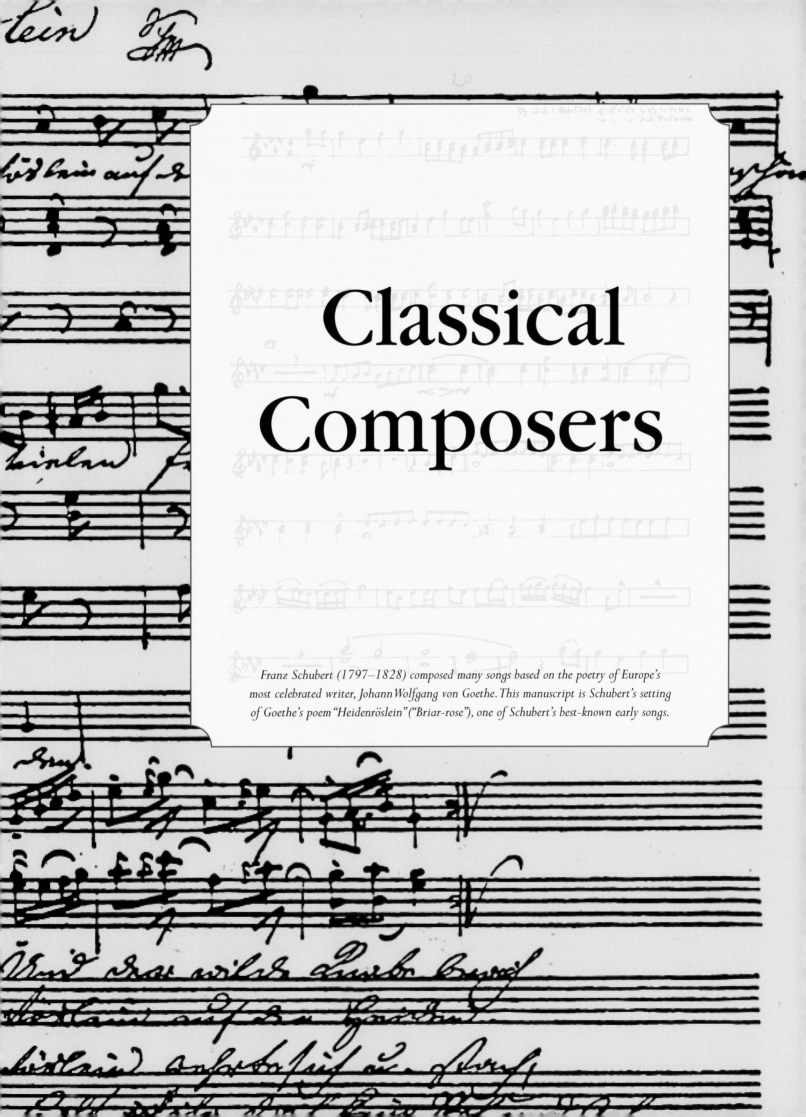

Classical Composers

Franz Schubert (1797–1828) composed many songs based on the poetry of Europe's most celebrated writer, Johann Wolfgang von Goethe. This manuscript is Schubert's setting of Goethe's poem "Heidenröslein" ("Briar-rose"), one of Schubert's best-known early songs.

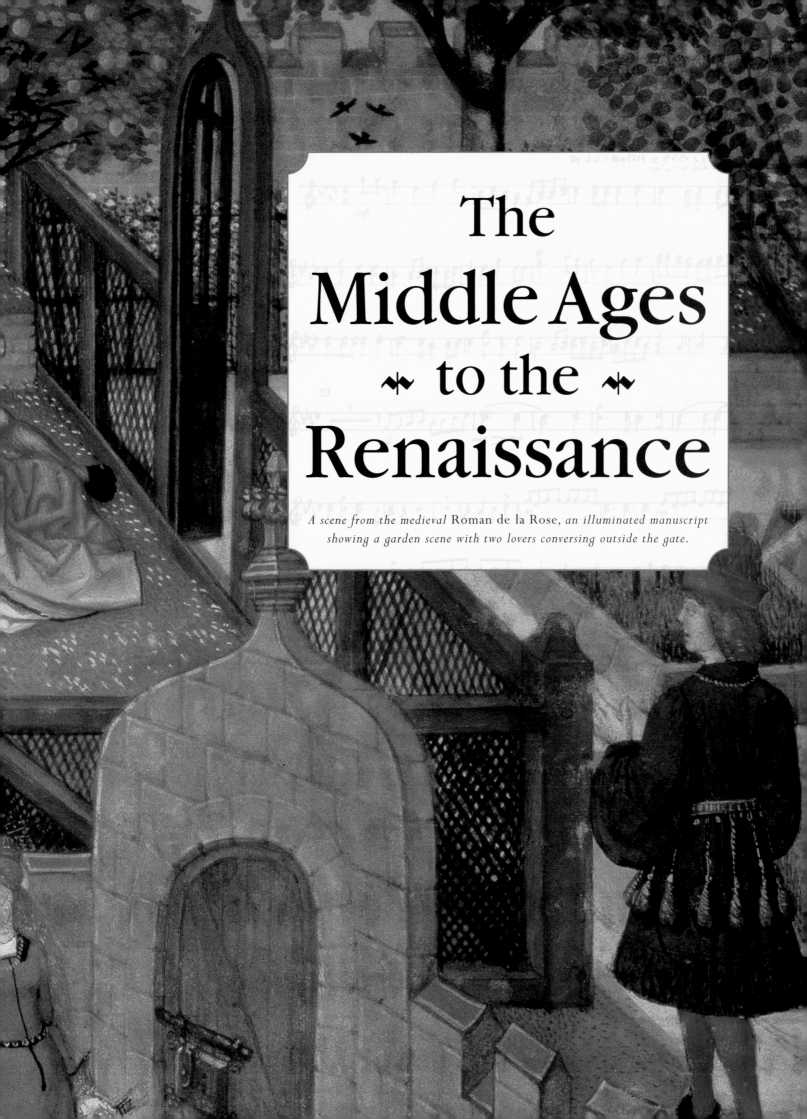

The Middle Ages to the Renaissance

A scene from the medieval Roman de la Rose, *an illuminated manuscript showing a garden scene with two lovers conversing outside the gate.*

Medieval and Polyphonic Music

*The sound of the cornet, flute, harp, sackbut, psaltery, dulcimer,
and all kinds of music.*

DANIEL, 3:3

Until the 20th century, there was a general perception that the history of music began with Bach. Only with the huge growth in musical research and scholarship, together with the explosion of the "early music movement" in the later decades of the 20th century, did many lost masterpieces of the medieval and Renaissance periods come to light, prompting a re-evaluation of their composers' achievements.

Sacred music

Music in the Middle Ages was largely the preserve of the church. Surviving medieval sources were mostly produced by monastic scribes, and kept in monastery libraries. While secular music existed, much of it was improvised,

ABOVE: *A page from an illuminated Flemish medieval psalter dating from c.1470.*

so the earliest music to survive was generally intended for sacred use.

The names of individual composers become scarcer the further back into history we travel. Among the earliest musicians who may be singled out from the 12th and early 13th centuries are the French composers Léonin and Pérotin, who were associated with the newly built cathedral of Notre-Dame in Paris. A spate of enormously popular recordings has recently revealed the visionary music of the 12th-century nun Hildegard of Bingen, who not only has the distinction of being one of the

earliest known composers, but was also a woman working in a field where women have traditionally not been prominent. She is now something of a feminist icon. Performances and recordings by early music groups have also uncovered a wealth of music by unnamed composers derived from medieval manuscript sources, such as the 13th-century Spanish *Cantigas* of Alfonso X.

Polyphony

The French composer Guillaume de Machaut was the single most important musical figure of the 14th century. His many innovations included being the first to compose a complete setting of the Ordinary of the Mass, the first to write music in four parts (which became the

ABOVE: *French church singers dating from the 14th century, the time of the innovative composer Guillaume de Machaut.*

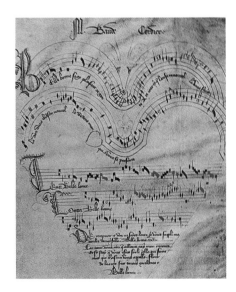

ABOVE: *A heart-shaped score, in red and black ink, of a three-part French chanson* Belle, bonne *by Baude Cordier (fl.1390s).*

such as Filippo Brunelleschi (1377–1446), evident in Florentine churches such as San Lorenzo and Santo Spirito, or the wonderful ducal palace at Urbino, found a musical counterpart in Renaissance polyphony. Music, too, acquired new depth and perspective. While three Flemish composers had dominated the 15th century, the polyphonic art of the High Renaissance was perfected by a trio of musicians – Palestrina from Italy, Lassus from Flanders, and Victoria from Spain – who all spent long periods in Italy.

The polyphonic principle continued to dominate 16th-century music, from the Masses and motets written for performance in the great Catholic churches of France, Italy, Spain and southern Germany, to the equivalent settings of both Catholic and Protestant liturgies by the English composers Tallis and Byrd, and the enchanting secular partsongs of the Elizabethan madrigal school. Meanwhile the plangent songs and solo lute music of Dowland looked forward to a new age of individualism.

ABOVE: An illumination from a 15th-century manuscript showing secular musicians playing a variety of instruments – crumhorn, fiddle, lute, bagpipes, nakers (drums) and triangle.

standard polyphonic combination), and one of the first to set the typical secular poetic forms of his day: *ballade*, *rondeau* and *virelay*.

For the next century, the musical centres of gravity remained the courts and churches of northern France and Flanders, which produced the sacred and secular works of the Flemish composers associated with the court of the dukes of Burgundy: Dufay, Ockeghem, Josquin des Prez and their contemporaries. However, many drew inspiration from prolonged visits to Italy, where musical activity flourished at important courts such as those of Ferrara and Mantua.

The harmonious exercises in perspective of Renaissance architects

ABOVE: The nave and choir of the church of Santo Spirito in Florence, designed by Filippo Brunelleschi in the mid 15th century. This church is a classic Renaissance masterpiece of perspective.

Hildegard of Bingen

A feather on the breath of God.

HILDEGARD

This remarkable woman was one of the earliest known composers. A contemporary of the famous medieval lovers Abélard and Héloïse, who also ended their lives in monastic institutions, Hildegard was born into a noble German family. As the tenth child she was considered a tithe and therefore due to the church, and was dedicated to religious service. When she was eight years old, she was sent as a novice to the Benedictine monastery of Disibodenberg.

In 1136 Hildegard became an abbess in her own right, and around the age of 50 she founded a nunnery near Bingen in the Rhine Valley. She died at the advanced age of 81, and her name was

ABOVE: An illustrated 13th-century manuscript depicting The Vision of St Hildegard, compiled 50 years after her death in 1179.

ABOVE: A modern plaque in the German town of Bingen commemorating its famous Abbess, Hildegard of Bingen.

put forward by several popes as a candidate for canonization. Though never formally canonized, she is often referred to as a saint, and has a feast-day which is particularly celebrated in Germany.

Mysticism and music

Hildegard was a visionary, and soon gained a widespread reputation as a prophetess. Popes, emperors, monarchs, archbishops and clergymen of all kinds flocked to Bingen to consult this "Sybil of the Rhine". Between 1141 and 1170 she recorded her mystical experiences; she also wrote two important works on natural history and medicine, and a great deal

of lyric and dramatic poetry, collected together in a volume called *Symphonia armonie celestium revelationum*.

Most of her poetry is liturgical, including antiphons, sequences and hymns designed for performance on the feast-days of particular saints. Among her work is the earliest known surviving morality play, *Ordo virtutum*, which describes the 16 Virtues battling with the Devil for a human soul. This and many of her poems have music attached, written in German neumatic notation. Unlike much music of this period, Hildegard's melodies are not drawn from monastic plainsong, but are strikingly original, and sometimes highly complex and decorative.

Many of her works have been performed and recorded during the recent revival of interest in early music: the album released under the title *A Feather on the Breath of God* (1984) has enjoyed huge popularity.

Life and works

NATIONALITY: German

BORN: Böckelheim, 1098;
DIED: Bingen, 1179

SPECIALIST GENRES: Plainsong settings of her own poetry.

MAJOR WORK: *Ordo virtutum*; *Symphonia armonie celestium revelationum*.

The Notre-Dame School

*Who could retain a grievance against the man
with whom he had joined in singing before God?*

St Ambrose (c.339–97)

Léonin and Pérotin – sometimes referred to as Master Leoninus and Master Perotinus – were the best-known of a group of composers who worked in medieval Paris in the late 12th and early 13th centuries. This was the age of King Philippe-Auguste (Philippe II), during whose reign, from 1180 to 1223, the medieval kingdom of France was consolidated. Little is known of the lives of Léonin and Pérotin, but both are associated with the cathedral of Notre-Dame de Paris, whose foundations were laid in the mid 1160s, and its high altar consecrated in 1182.

Léonin

The major work attributed to Léonin was the *Magnus liber* ("great book") designed for use by the choir of the new cathedral. He is mentioned by an anonymous 13th-century theorist as "the best composer of organum for the amplification of divine service",

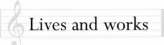

ABOVE: An initial letter from an illuminated French psalter dating from the 13th century – the time of Léonin and Pérotin.

suggesting that he wrote polyphonic settings for two independent voices of parts of the liturgy intended for performance on the main feast-days of the church's year. Léonin may also have been among the first to indicate rhythm as well as pitch in his musical notation. His vocal writing was imaginative, free-flowing and improvisatory in style.

Pérotin

Some time after Léonin's death, Pérotin, who may have been his pupil, seems to have revised and shortened the *Magnus liber*. Pérotin remains a shadowy figure. He may have been born around 1160, and died some time between 1205 and 1225. Some scholars have suggested that he may

have worked at the royal parish church of St Germain-l'Auxerrois, near the Tuileries Palace, since there is no direct evidence that he worked at Notre-Dame.

Pérotin was active in the creation of the four-voice motet, an ecclesiastical musical form which survives to the present day. His contribution towards the development of three- and four-voice polyphony was one of the most important steps forward in musical history. Of his works, two graduals in four voices for the Christmas season survive, as do about a dozen liturgical works in three voices, and about 160 *clausulae* – polyphonic passages written for insertion into liturgical plainsong to vary the texture.

ABOVE: A view of medieval Paris showing the cathedral of Notre-Dame, where Léonin and Pérotin worked, from the 15th-century Book of Hours of Etienne Chevalier.

Lives and works

Nationality: French

Active: Léonin, c.1163–90; Pérotin, c.1200

Specialist genres: Early polyphonic sacred music.

Major works: *Magnus liber*, motets and graduals.

Guillaume de Machaut

*...the morning star of song, who made
his music heard below.*

ALFRED, LORD TENNYSON (1809–92), "A DREAM OF FAIR WOMEN"

A near contemporary of Geoffrey Chaucer (c.1340–1400), whose poetry he influenced, Guillaume de Machaut was one of the most important composers of the 14th century. Not only did he compose more than anyone else of his period, but his works are enormously varied in style and form.

He seems to have spent much of his life in Rheims, in northern France, where he died. He entered the service of John, King of Bohemia, around 1323, and in the manner of a courtier of the time, travelled around Europe in the royal retinue until the king was killed at the Battle of Crécy in 1346. Meanwhile, however, John's patronage had enabled Machaut to procure

ABOVE: A contemporary portrait of Guillaume de Machaut (1300–77), one of the earliest surviving portraits of a composer.

several lucrative canonries at major northern French cathedrals. After John's death, Machaut continued to serve the French nobility, including the future King Charles V (for whose coronation he composed a Mass) and John, Duke of Berry.

Ars nova

Machaut's output is equally divided between sacred and secular music. His most famous piece is the *Notre-Dame Mass*, and he wrote over 20 motets, but also a large quantity of secular songs – ballades, rondeaux and virelays, which were the principal vocal types of the time. His works are representative of the French *ars nova*, or new style, and are often very rhythmically complex.

ABOVE: A joust, watched by ladies. Many of Machaut's songs dealt with courtly love.

Life and works

NATIONALITY: French

BORN: Machaut, c.1300;
DIED: Rheims, 1377

SPECIALIST GENRES: Sacred and secular vocal music of the *ars nova.*

MAJOR WORKS: *Notre-Dame Mass*; motets; secular songs.

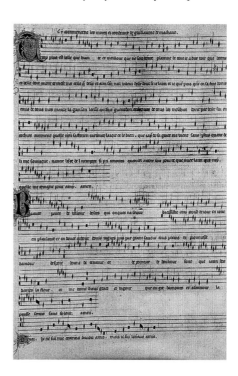

ABOVE: The score of a Machaut motet, an example of the 14th-century ars nova *style.*

Guillaume Dufay

L'homme armé doibt on doubter. (Fear the armed man.)

ANONYMOUS, 15TH-CENTURY FOLK SONG

The pre-eminence of northern France and Flanders in the development of compositional technique continued into the 15th century, in the person of Guillaume Dufay. Born near Brussels around the turn of the century, the illegitimate son of a priest, he became a choirboy at Cambrai Cathedral and, around 1420, he entered the service of the powerful Italian Malatesta family. He seems to have returned from Italy to hold posts in several churches in and around Cambrai in the mid 1420s, but in 1428 he became a singer in the papal choir in Rome. While in Italy, he evidently worked for several other noble families, including the Este family of Ferrara and the dukes of Savoy. He returned north to Cambrai around 1436, when he became a canon at the cathedral, but he maintained his ties with Italy, spending seven years in Savoy in the 1450s. He died at Cambrai and was buried in a chapel in the cathedral.

ABOVE: Guillaume Dufay depicted in a French manuscript dating from 1440 called Le champion des dames.

Cantus firmus

Dufay was the most celebrated composer of his time: other budding composers flocked to Cambrai to seek his advice. His surviving compositions – about 200 in all – show his absolute mastery of the major forms of his time, together with an attractive and fluent talent for melody. Many of his works are harmonizations of liturgical chants, but eight complete Masses survive, along with Mass fragments, hymns, antiphons and motets. Many of his works are based on a *cantus firmus* – either a plainsong melody or a popular secular tune, such as the folk song *L'homme armé* (*The Armed Man*), on which Dufay based his most famous Mass. (The same tune was used in this way by many other composers of the 15th, 16th and 17th centuries.) Dufay also wrote over 80 songs – probably for his Italian patrons – for voices accompanied by instruments. He was apparently the first to write a Requiem Mass, completed just four years before his own death, but the manuscript of this work has been lost.

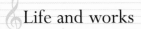

Life and works

NATIONALITY: Flemish

BORN: near Brussels, 1397; **DIED:** Cambrai, 1474

SPECIALIST GENRES: Polyphonic sacred and secular forms.

MAJOR WORKS: Motets; Masses; songs.

ABOVE: A Dance of the Shepherds *depicted in a 15th-century Book of Hours (of Charles d'Angoulême), now held in the Bibliothèque Nationale in Paris.*

Johannes Ockeghem

He alone of all singers is free from all vice and abounds in all virtues.

Among the composers who visited Dufay at Cambrai was the Franco-Flemish composer Johannes (or Jean d') Ockeghem, then aged around 50, and destined to succeed Dufay as the most celebrated composer of his period.

Ockeghem's early life, and even his birthplace and date, are shrouded in obscurity. The earliest mention of him is as a singer at Notre-Dame in Antwerp in 1443; shortly afterwards he entered the service of Charles I, Duke of Bourbon, at Moulins in France. In the early 1450s he was employed by Charles VII of France as a chaplain, and probably remained in the royal service until his death. He died at an advanced age in Tours, where he had been for many years, and by royal appointment, treasurer of St Martin's Church. He appears to have been admired as much for the kindness and generosity of his character as for the "extraordinary sweetness and beauty" of his music, and his death was mourned in flowery verbal and musical tributes from fellow musicians and poets.

ABOVE: Johannes Ockeghem directing a choir of monks in the Gloria of one of his Masses.

Contrapuntal innovation

Relatively few of Ockeghem's compositions have survived, among them 14 Masses, a polyphonic Requiem Mass (which is the earliest surviving example), nine motets and a handful of secular chansons. His Masses are the most important of their time. The earlier ones are based, like Dufay's, on an existing melody, either sacred or secular; but the later ones are more experimental. Instead of keeping the *cantus firmus* in the tenor part, Ockeghem shares it between the voices, producing a texture of great contrapuntal complexity. He was also the first composer known to have used the melodies of his own songs as the *cantus firmus* of a Mass setting (a technique known as "parody mass", used in his Masses *Fors seulement*, *Au travail suis* and *Ma maistresse*). Several of his works, notably the *Missa prolationum*, do not rely on a *cantus firmus*, but are freely constructed from an intricate combination of rhythmic and melodic fragments.

ABOVE: Ockeghem's last royal patron, Charles VIII of France (reigned 1477–98). He had worked for three French kings.

Life and works

NATIONALITY: Flemish

BORN: ?Dender, c.1410; **DIED:** Tours, 1497

SPECIALIST GENRES: Polyphonic sacred works.

MAJOR WORKS: 14 Masses.

Josquin des Prez

Josquin is master of the notes; others are mastered by them.

MARTIN LUTHER (1483–1546)

Among the tributes paid to Ockeghem was the beautiful elegy *Nymphes des bois*, written by the final member of the great 15th-century trio of Franco-Flemish composers. Josquin des Prez, who may have been Ockeghem's pupil, can lay claim to being the finest composer of the High Renaissance. Possibly born in Picardy, he may have begun his career as a choirboy in the collegiate church at St Quentin, but then went to Milan, where he sang in the cathedral choir and also worked for the Sforza family.

In the late 1480s he was a member of the papal choir. Around 1500 he was working both for the French court and for the dukes of Ferrara, but when plague broke out in Ferrara in 1503 he fled north, becoming provost of the church of Notre-Dame in Condé. He died there in August 1521 and was

ABOVE: *A woodcut of Josquin des Prez (c.1440–1521).*

commemorated by a flood of verbal and musical homages. Josquin's fame as a composer during his lifetime is attested by three individual publications of his Masses in the

early 1500s by the Venetian printer Petrucci. Publications devoted to the works of one composer were extremely rare at the time.

Matching music to words

Like Mozart some three centuries later, Josquin took the common musical currency of his time and refined it into pure gold. He was one of the first composers to relate his music closely to the text: his word-setting is infinitely sensitive, dramatic and highly expressive, while his use of complex musical techniques is handled in a masterly but unobtrusive way. His early Masses were based on *cantus firmus* techniques, but the later ones, such as *Ave Maris Stella*, *L'homme armé* and *Pange lingua*, use a variety of unifying devices including parody technique and motto themes.

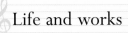

Life and works

NATIONALITY: Flemish

BORN: ?Picardy, c.1440; DIED: Condé, 1521

SPECIALIST GENRES: Polyphonic sacred works and secular songs.

MAJOR WORKS: 19 Masses, including *Pange lingua* and *De beata virgine*.

ABOVE: *A page from a 16th-century missal showing part of Josquin's Mass* Pange lingua *(Sing, my tongue).*

Giovanni Pierluigi da Palestrina

The most frivolous and gallant words are set to exactly the same music as those of the Bible…
the truth is that he could not write any other kind of music.

HECTOR BERLIOZ (1803–69), "MEMOIRS"

Palestrina's name has become synonymous with textbook perfection in the field of harmony and counterpoint, and his reputation long outlived him. He began his career in Rome as organist and choir-master.

In 1552, under the patronage of his former bishop, now Pope Julius III, Palestrina became choir-master at the Julian Chapel, the training school for the Sistine Choir. After three years he was dismissed by a new pope because he was married, but in the same year he succeeded Lassus as choir-master of the church of St John Lateran. He resigned after a dispute over money matters in 1560, and returned to S. Maria Maggiore, but during the last two decades of his life he worked once more at the Julian Chapel.

In the 1570s Palestrina lost his brother, two of his sons, and finally his wife in plague epidemics, which led him to consider entering the

ABOVE: A contemporary painting of Giovanni Pierluigi da Palestrina, who worked mostly in Rome.

ABOVE: An artist's impression of Palestrina at work, composing one of his many Masses.

priesthood. However, in 1581, just eight months after his first wife's death, he married a wealthy widow, who assured his financial security.

Masses and motets

Palestrina worked against the background of the Counter-Reformation. The Council of Trent had initiated ecclesiastical reforms, which decreed that sacred music should be kept simple so that the words could be heard clearly. Elaborate polyphony and the extensive use of instrumental accompaniment was discouraged. Palestrina's Masses and motets are all constructed with an ear to clarity of textual declamation: the vocal lines flow freely and the intertwining parts create their own beauty, enhancing rather than obscuring the meaning of the words.

Over 100 of Palestrina's Masses survive, including the famous *Missa Papae Marcelli*, together with about 375 motets for between four and 12 voices and many other liturgical works, including Magnificat and Lamentation settings. However, as his career demonstrates, he achieved a balance between the sacred and the secular. While much of his music was written to the glory of God, some is based on secular models; and his many published collections include two books of madrigals.

Life and works

NATIONALITY: Italian

BORN: Palestrina, c.1525; **DIED:** Rome, 1594

SPECIALIST GENRES: Polyphonic sacred music.

MAJOR WORKS: *Missa Papae Marcelli* (1567); *Missa Assumpta est Maria* (1567); *Missa brevis* (1570); Stabat Mater (1590).

Orlande de Lassus

Orlandissimo Lassissimo amorevolissimo.

LASSUS'S SIGNATURE ON A LETTER TO DUKE WILHELM V, C.1575

The Flemish composer Orlande de Lassus (sometimes known by the Italian form of his name, Orlando di Lasso) was a contemporary of Palestrina: they died in the same year. Lassus spent his early years travelling in Sicily and Italy attached to the households of various Italian nobles. His earliest collections of compositions – madrigals, songs and motets – were published in Antwerp and Venice when he was in his early 20s, and in 1556 he joined the court of Duke Albrecht V of Bavaria in Munich, as a singer in the ducal chapel.

Court music

By 1563 Lassus had risen to become the duke's *maestro di cappella*, a position he held until his death. His duties

ABOVE: The Flemish composer Orlande de Lassus (c.1532–94), painted in 1580 by Johann von Achen.

included providing sacred music for the chapel's services, and secular music for the court's entertainment on occasions such as state visits, banquets and hunting parties. In 1569 he provided the music for the sumptuous festivities surrounding the marriage of Duke Wilhelm V of Bavaria to Renée of Lorraine. Lassus continued to travel widely, particularly in France and Italy, but his base remained Munich for the last 34 years of his life, towards the end of which he suffered from

depression and became preoccupied with sacred works. Two of his sons became musicians. His own fame had spread far and wide, and he was one of the most respected and prolific composers of his time. About 2000 of his compositions survive.

His supreme mastery of the art of polyphony is demonstrated in his Masses, motets, settings of the Passions and other liturgical works, including the fine *Psalmi Davidis poenitentiales* (*Seven Penitential Psalms of David*) published in 1584 but written around 1563. He was equally skilled in the lighter, more lyrical style, exemplified in his Italianate madrigals and French chansons.

ABOVE: The Royal Chapel in Munich, c.1565, where Lassus worked as maestro di cappella. *He is the bearded figure dressed in yellow.*

Life and works

NATIONALITY: Flemish

BORN: Mons, c.1532;
DIED: Munich, 1594

SPECIALIST GENRES:
Polyphonic sacred and lyrical secular music.

MAJOR WORKS: *Psalmi Davidis poenitentiales* (1584); "Tristis est anima mea" (1568); "Adoremus te, Christe" (1604) and many other motets.

Tomás Luis de Victoria

...in solemn beauty like slow old tunes of Spain.

JOHN MASEFIELD (1878–1967)

Victoria (also known as Tommaso Ludovico da Vittoria) stands beside Palestrina and Lassus as one of the finest composers of the 16th century. He was born into a distinguished family in Ávila, where he was a choirboy at the cathedral (one of his uncles was a canon there), and attended a highly regarded Jesuit school. In 1563 he was sent to the Jesuit Collegio Germanico in Rome, where he may have studied composition with Palestrina. Eight years later he himself became a music teacher there, finally leaving in early 1577, by which time he had been

ABOVE: *The title page of a book of Tomás Luis de Victoria's motets, published in 1589 as* Cantiones sacrae *(Sacred Songs).*

ordained as a priest. He took up a chaplaincy at San Girolamo della Carità, but also drew income from five benefices back in Spain, granted to him by Pope Gregory XIII.

Madrid

In the early 1580s Victoria decided that he wanted to return to Spain, and King Philip II appointed him chaplain to his sister, the Dowager Empress Maria, at the Madrid convent where she lived. Victoria served the empress from 1587 until her death in 1603, and subsequently remained at the convent until his own death, refusing many tempting offers from other Spanish cathedrals. From 1592–5 he revisited Rome to supervise the printing of a book of Masses, and also attended Palestrina's funeral.

Though Victoria wrote only sacred music, as befitted his priestly vocation, his works are far from solemn, revealing a naturally sunny disposition. His 20 Masses were all published in his lifetime: many of them are based on his own motets, antiphons and psalms, while the *Missa pro victoria* is a battle Mass based on a popular French chanson called *La guerre* (*The War*). There are also 16 extant Magnificat settings, many other shorter liturgical works, and a much-admired sequence of music for Holy Week, including nine expressive Lamentations.

ABOVE: *King Philip II of Spain (1527–98), painted c.1575.*

Life and works

NATIONALITY: Spanish

BORN: Ávila, c.1548;
DIED: Madrid, 1611

SPECIALIST GENRES:
Richly polyphonic
sacred works.

MAJOR WORK:
Requiem Mass for the
Dowager Empress Maria
(1603); 20 Masses;
16 Magnificats.

Thomas Tallis

As he did live, so also did he die,
In mild and quiet sort (O! happy man)

TALLIS'S EPITAPH

During his long and productive lifetime, the English composer Thomas Tallis served four monarchs: Henry VIII, Edward VI, Mary Tudor and Elizabeth I. Though born a Catholic, he managed to survive an extremely dangerous age of religious upheaval and persecution, mainly by adapting his musical style to suit the circumstances, and by keeping a low personal profile.

Royal monopoly

Probably a native of Kent, Tallis's first recorded post was as organist of the Benedictine Priory in Dover. He then joined the choir of Waltham Abbey, near London, around 1538. The Abbey was dissolved in 1540, during Henry VIII's reign, and Tallis became a lay clerk at Canterbury Cathedral. From around 1543 until his death he shared the position of organist and composer to the Chapel Royal with his pupil, William Byrd.

ABOVE: *Thomas Tallis shared with Byrd the right to print music and music paper.*

In 1575 Tallis and Byrd received a patent from Elizabeth I granting them a 21-year monopoly on printing music and music paper in England. Their first publication was a joint collection of 34 *Cantiones sacrae* (sacred songs) in five and six parts.

Textual clarity

Tallis is chiefly remembered for his church music, setting text in both Latin and English, depending on the prevailing religious climate. One notable feature of his style was a move away from florid, elaborate counterpoint towards simpler, syllabic declamation in which the text could be clearly heard: in this respect he was pointing the way forward to the Baroque era.

His mastery of contrapuntal techniques is amply demonstrated in his breathtaking 40-part motet *Spem in alium*, which opens in 20-part imitation. The hymn tune known as "Tallis's Canon" (later set as a hymn tune to the words "Glory to thee, my God, this night") was written for Archbishop Parker's *Metrical Psalter* of 1567, and another tune was used by Vaughan Williams as the basis for his *Fantasia on a Theme of Thomas Tallis* (1910).

LEFT: *Queen Elizabeth I, by George Gower (1540–96). During the Elizabethan period (1558–1603) Tallis wrote his later works, such as the Whitsuntide anthem O Lord give Thy Holy Spirit.*

Life and works

NATIONALITY: English

BORN: ?Kent, c.1505;
DIED: Greenwich, 1585

SPECIALIST GENRES:
Polyphonic motets in Latin and English.

MAJOR WORKS: Motet *Spem in alium* (c.1570); *Lamentations of Jeremiah; Cantiones sacrae.*

William Byrd

How daintily this Byrd his notes doth vary,
As if he were the Nightingale's own brother.

<small>ANONYMOUS, FROM THE PREFACE TO "PARTHENIA", 1613</small>

Apart from Tallis, the other giant of 16th-century English music was his pupil, William Byrd. In 1563, aged about 20, Byrd was appointed organist and master of the choristers at Lincoln Cathedral. He married in 1568 and had several children. In 1570 he became a Gentleman of the Chapel Royal in London, while also making the acquaintance of various powerful nobles, to whom he dedicated compositions.

Catholicism

His noble patrons undoubtedly helped to protect Byrd through difficult times, when he became known as a Roman Catholic recusant and continued to risk prosecution by writing Masses for undercover use by prominent Catholic families. His three fine Latin Masses, in four, three and five parts respectively, were published openly in the 1590s, but after his publication between

ABOVE: William Byrd was a Catholic composer who managed to survive persecution at the time of Elizabeth I.

1605–10 of the *Gradualia* (a huge collection of music for use with the Catholic liturgy), possession of the volume became a criminal offence.

Songs and instrumental music

Between 1588 and 1611, Byrd published three collections of *Psalmes, Songs and Sonnets*, miscellaneous collections of English anthems, secular partsongs, madrigals and pieces for viol consort. His instrumental music was particularly fine: he was a master of the art of consort music (particularly fantasias for viols), and of keyboard music, especially the pavans and galliards so much loved by Queen Elizabeth I and her court. His keyboard music

appeared in various collections intended for aristocratic use, including the *Fitzwilliam Virginal Book, My Lady Nevell's Book* and *Parthenia*, a printed collection issued in 1613 jointly with John Bull (1563–1628) and Orlando Gibbons (1583–1625). Byrd's later years were spent at an Essex mansion, where he died. His Latin church music lay forgotten until the mid 19th century, although his Anglican anthems remained constantly popular. His madrigals and lively keyboard music were rediscovered in the early 20th century. At least two of the English madrigalists were his pupils, and his influence on English music was profound.

ABOVE: A magnificently inlaid virginal, once owned by Queen Elizabeth I. Byrd wrote a great deal of virginal music.

Life and works

NATIONALITY: English

BORN: ?Lincoln, c.1543;
DIED: Stonden Massey, Essex, 1623

SPECIALIST GENRES: Sacred music, songs, madrigals, keyboard works, consort pieces for viols.

MAJOR WORKS: Masses, three Latin and one English; *Cantiones sacrae* (1575); 140 keyboard pieces, including *The Queenes Alman* and *Wolsey's Wilde*.

Carlo Gesualdo

...music oft hath such a charm
To make bad good, and good provoke to harm.

WILLIAM SHAKESPEARE (1564–1616), "MEASURE FOR MEASURE"

Gesualdo, Prince of Venosa, occupies a unique place in the history of music: he was both a composer (albeit an amateur one) and a murderer. He came of an aristocratic Neapolitan family: his mother was a niece of Pope Pius IV and the sister of a prominent cardinal, and his uncle was Archbishop of Naples – a potent and dangerous brew of religion and politics which characterized the highest levels of contemporary Italian society.

Scandal

In 1586, after the death of his elder brother left Gesualdo heir to the family title, he married his beautiful cousin Maria d'Avalos, daughter of the Marquis of Pescara. Four years later he caught his wife with her aristocratic lover and had them both stabbed to death. The double murder caused a storm of protest, and Gesualdo retired to his country estates, and devoted himself to composition.

ABOVE: Carlo Gesualdo, Prince of Venosa (kneeling), with his uncle, Carlo Borromeo, Archbishop of Naples.

In 1594 he visited Ferrara, where he married Leonora d'Este, the niece of Alfonso, Duke of Ferrara. This second marriage also proved unsuccessful.

Leonora soon tired of her gloomy husband's introspective and melancholy nature, and after their only son died in childhood, Gesualdo increasingly withdrew from the world. He died on the edge of madness, a lonely and embittered man.

Harmony and dissonance

Gesualdo's place in musical history is assured by his six collections of madrigals. Many of these illustrate dolorous texts (containing many references to pain, death and sorrow) with extraordinarily advanced chromatic harmony – perhaps reflecting his tortured mental state. Four centuries later, Gesualdo's love of dissonant harmony excited the interest of Stravinsky; but he had little immediate influence, being seen as an extreme example of the "mannerist" style in music. Nevertheless, he is one of the composers who bridged the divide between Renaissance and Baroque.

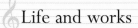

Life and works

NATIONALITY: Italian

BORN: Naples, c.1560;
DIED: Naples, 1613

SPECIALIST GENRES:
Secular vocal
music.

MAJOR WORKS: Six
books of madrigals.

ABOVE: A painting showing the view of the shoreline at Naples, by Gaspar van Wittel (1653–1736), now in the Palazzo Pitti in Florence.

English Madrigal School

He would sing of her with falls
Used in lovely madrigals.

<small>ELIZABETH BARRETT BROWNING (1806–61), "A PORTRAIT"</small>

The madrigal – a setting of a (usually secular) text for several voices – developed in Italy towards the end of the 13th century, but flowered some 300 years later in the hands of both Flemish and Italian composers, including Gesualdo and Luca Marenzio (1553–99). During the reign of Elizabeth I (1558–1603) this immensely popular form was imported to England by Italian composers working at the English court. The publication in 1588 of the Italian collection *Musica transalpina* inspired native composers to follow the Italian example.

Thomas Morley

Among these was Byrd's pupil, Thomas Morley (1557–1602), who may have been a friend of Shakespeare (his famous setting of "It was a Lover and his Lass" was probably written for the original production of *As You Like It* in 1599). In 1601 Morley edited *The Triumphs of Oriana*, a celebrated anthology of madrigals by the best composers of the time in honour of the Queen, to which he himself contributed "Arise, Awake" and "Hard by a Crystal Fountain".

ABOVE: An English masque at the time of Elizabeth I, with musicians playing lute, viols, gittern and flute, and singing madrigals.

Thomas Weelkes

Morley's friend Thomas Weelkes (c.1576–1623) was another contributor to the same anthology (with the madrigal "As Vesta was from Latmos Hill Descending"). He was an

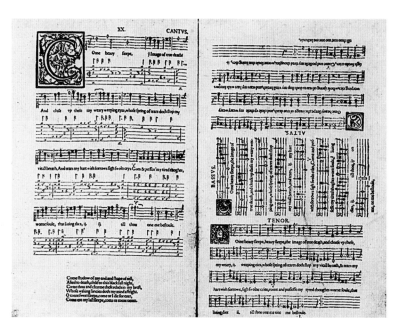

ABOVE: One of John Dowland's songs, from The First Booke of Songes or Ayres of Foure Partes, *with tablature for the lute (1597).*

organist and composer, who published three books of madrigals between 1597 and 1600. His accomplished compositions include "O Care, Thou Wilt Despatch Me", "Thule, the Period of Cosmography" and "Like Two Proud Armies", as well as some fine church music.

John Wilbye

Wilbye (1574–1638) published two madrigal collections in 1598 and 1614; he is regarded as one of the greatest exponents of the genre. His madrigals include the powerfully expressive "Draw on, Sweet Night", "Sweet Honey-sucking Bees" and "Weep, Weep, Mine Eyes".

John Dowland

At the same time, the solo song with lute accompaniment was coming into its own in England. Dowland (c.1563–1626), its finest exponent, was the royal lutenist to the court of James I. Among his greatest works are the affecting songs "Flow my Tears", "Sweet, Stay Awhile" and "In Darkness Let Me Dwell", together with his 1604 collection of lute pieces *Lachrimae* (*Tears*).

Other Composers of the Era

Modern church music is so constructed that
the congregation cannot hear one distinct word.

DESIDERIUS ERASMUS (1466–1536)

Many composers made outstanding contributions to the development and vitality of polyphonic music during this period. Notable for his chansons and motets, Gilles Binchois (c.1400–60) was organist at Mons Cathedral, and a member of the Burgundian court chapel from 1430. He may also have served as a soldier, fighting with the occupying English army at the time of Joan of Arc. His death was lamented in works by both Ockeghem and Dufay (in a rondeau – a form much cultivated by Binchois). His secular songs embody the courtly tradition of the time, and his sacred music represents a consolidation of the Burgundian style.

Binchois's contemporary, John Dunstable (c.1390–1453), was the leading English composer of his time. Also an astrologer and mathematician,

ABOVE: Gilles Binchois (right) with his great contemporary and fellow composer Guillaume Dufay, c.1440.

Dunstable travelled widely in Europe in the service of his aristocratic patrons, and enjoyed an international reputation. He was a master of isorhythmic technique, and his Masses and motets greatly influenced Dufay.

The 15th-century Flemish composer Jacob Obrecht (c.1451–1505) divided his time between the Netherlands and Ferrara, where he died of the plague. He often used secular tunes as the basis for his Masses and motets (a technique he bequeathed to Josquin des Prez), and was one of the first known composers to employ number symbolism in his music.

Antiphony
Another Flemish-born composer, Adriaan Willaert (c.1490–1562), played a significant role in the transition between Renaissance and

Baroque styles. One of the earliest madrigal composers, he became choir-master at St Mark's in Venice in 1527, where he established the principle of writing antiphonal music for double choirs, a form well suited to the special acoustic properties of the Byzantine-style basilica.

Willaert's work greatly influenced Giovanni Gabrieli (1557–1612), who became organist at St Mark's in 1585, inheriting the post from his uncle Andrea (c.1510–86), who had been Willaert's pupil. Giovanni initiated the tradition of writing Venetian motets with instrumental accompaniment. He perfected antiphonal technique both in his motets and his purely instrumental music. The first set of his *Sacrae symphoniae*, 1597, contains the famous *Sonata pian' e forte* for groups of brass instruments.

ABOVE: The English Agincourt Song, celebrating Henry V's victory at Agincourt (1415), dating from the time of Dunstable.

ABOVE: The Flemish composer Adriaan Willaert, who served as music director at St Mark's Cathedral, Venice, for over 30 years.

The Middle Ages to the Renaissance **35**

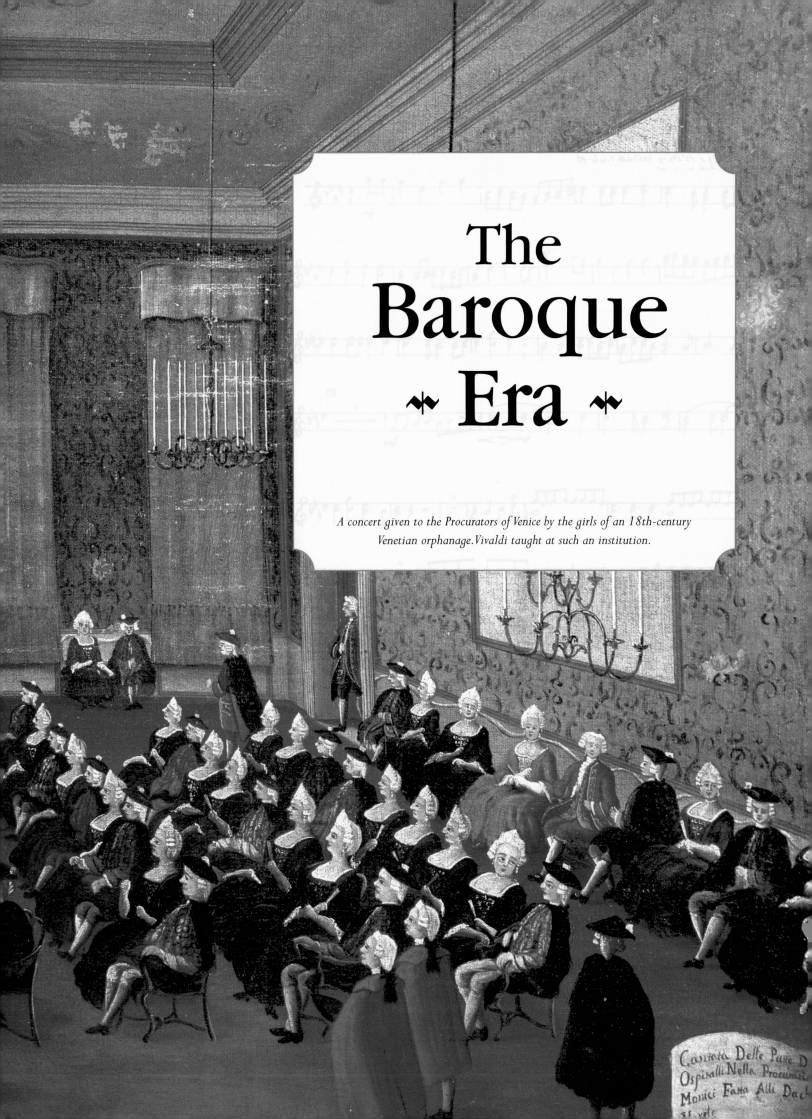

The Baroque ❧ Era ❧

A concert given to the Procurators of Venice by the girls of an 18th-century Venetian orphanage. Vivaldi taught at such an institution.

Harmony and Ornament

Architecture in general is frozen music.

FRIEDRICH VON SCHELLING (1775–1854)

The term "Baroque", which is derived from *barroco*, the Portuguese word for a misshapen pearl, was originally used – in a pejorative sense – to describe the flamboyant, ornate architecture found in German, Austrian and Italian churches of the 17th century, which were designed as a reaction to the cool classicism of Renaissance architecture. One of the most prominent Baroque architects was the Italian sculptor Gianlorenzo Bernini (1598–1680), who worked principally in Rome. His work exhibits the fluid, dynamic shapes, theatricality and illusion that characterize the style.

In music, the Baroque period covers the years from c.1600–1750, during which Renaissance polyphony gave way to a new, highly ornamental style with a strong harmonic basis. Most Baroque music – from operatic arias to *concerti*

ABOVE: Baroque flamboyance at its height – the interior of St Peter's Basilica in Rome in 1730.

grossi for groups of instruments – was supported by a *basso continuo*, a firm bass line played on keyboard and reinforced on cello or bass, which provided a harmonic foundation.

Opera

The Baroque period saw the introduction of several new forms, mostly developed in Italy. In the late 16th century, a group of poets and musicians formed an association in Florence called the Camerata, and several of their members – the poet Ottavio Rinuccini (1562–1621) and the composers Jacopo Peri (1561–1633) and Giulio Caccini (c.1550–1618) – collaborated to produce

the earliest music-dramas, or operas. The new form was taken up and transformed by the genius of Claudio Monteverdi, whose three surviving operas are the earliest still to be regularly performed today.

Opera spread like wildfire, with demand coming not only from aristocratic patrons, but also from newly opened public opera houses. Monteverdi's pioneering work was carried on by composers such as Vivaldi and Alessandro Scarlatti in Italy, Hasse in Germany, Lully, Charpentier and Rameau in France, and the German-born Handel in England. Alongside secular operas (usually based on plots derived from ancient history or mythology), a similar sacred form – oratorio – developed, using the same forms and styles as opera, but based on biblical stories. Oratorio flourished both in the Catholic South and the

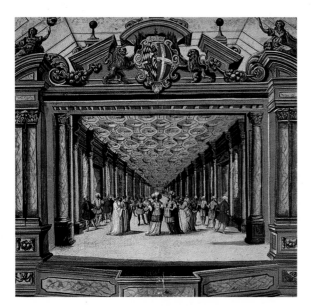

ABOVE: An opera theatre in Munich, Germany, in 1665.

Bach and Handel

In musical terms, the Baroque era reached its height in the works of Bach and Handel. Both were reared in the German Protestant tradition, but their careers took very different paths.

Bach concentrated on church music, whether for voices and instruments (in the form of the church cantata, a kind of unstaged mini-drama performed during the Sunday services), or for instruments alone (particularly solo organ). His Passion settings brought a German tradition to its peak, and his monumental Mass in B minor took the form to an unprecedented level.

Handel flourished in a more cosmopolitan environment, first in Italy and then in England, where he stepped neatly into the void left by the early death of Henry Purcell. Handel's many Italian operas, written for London theatres, have recently resumed their place in the repertoire, while his English oratorios have always been a well-loved feature of the British choral tradition.

ABOVE: A realistic depiction of an 18th-century private concert against an allegorical background, one of a set of four Fine Arts designs by Giuseppe Zocchi (1711–67).

Protestant North, where Heinrich Schütz pioneered it in Germany, paving the way for the great sacred works of J. S. Bach. It reached its apogee in the works of Handel, written in English, of which *Messiah* has been the most frequently performed.

Instrumental forms

The Baroque period also saw a huge demand for instrumental music, particularly concertos, *concerti grossi*, sonatas and suites, and almost all major composers worked in these new forms. Again, they flourished in Italy in the hands of Corelli, Vivaldi and Alessandro Scarlatti, but were equally popular in Germany. Bach's *Brandenburg Concertos* and Handel's sets of *concerti grossi* brought the genre to its peak, while the solo concerto and solo sonata underwent further metamorphosis in the Classical era. Meanwhile Alessandro Scarlatti's son Domenico, an exact contemporary of Bach and Handel, defied convention by removing to the Portuguese and Spanish courts, where he developed his own highly individual form of keyboard sonata.

ABOVE: The Rehearsal, *with viols, flute, oboe and voice, by Etienne Jeaurat (1699–1789).*

Claudio Monteverdi

Claudio Monteverdi, in moving the affections...
becomes the most pleasant tyrant of human minds.

Monteverdi was a composer of enormous significance in the history of music. Like his contemporary Heinrich Schütz in Germany, he bridged the worlds of the High Renaissance and the Baroque era. He can also be compared to Stravinsky: during the course of long lives both men showed an endless capacity to re-invent and adapt their musical styles according to changing tastes.

Early years

Monteverdi began his career as a chorister at the cathedral in his birthplace, Cremona. By the age of 16 – already a fine instrumentalist – he had published a volume of three-part motets and a book of sacred madrigals. In 1587 he published his first volume of secular madrigals, followed by a second volume in 1590. Around that time he found a job as a string player at the ducal court in Mantua, and by the

ABOVE: Claudio Monteverdi (1567–1643), painted around 1640 by Bernardo Strozzi.

time his third madrigal collection appeared in 1592 his fame as a composer was spreading rapidly. He married in 1599 and had three

children, of whom two sons survived: the elder became a musician, the younger a doctor.

Triumph and tragedy

In 1601 Monteverdi became *maestro di cappella* at the Mantuan court, where he published two more madrigal collections over the next four years. In 1607 he made his first foray into the new genre of opera with *L'Orfeo*, which was performed in Mantua in February. Seven months later his wife died after a long illness, leaving Monteverdi a grief-stricken widower with two small children.

He was obliged to pull himself together enough to finish his second opera, *L'Arianna*, which was performed in May 1608 to celebrate the marriage of the Gonzaga heir, Francesco, to Margaret of Savoy. (Only one aria from this opera has survived.) During rehearsals another tragedy struck when Caterina Martinelli, the young principal singer and a close friend of Monteverdi, died of smallpox. Monteverdi then suffered a complete collapse, although his glorious setting for voices and instruments of the *Vespro della beata vergine* (*Vespers of the Blessed Virgin*, 1610) dates from this unhappy period.

Venice

After making several attempts to leave the service of the Gonzagas, Monteverdi was finally dismissed in

ABOVE: The interior of the Teatro Olimpico in Vicenza, designed by Andrea Palladio (1508–80).

ABOVE: A scene from a 1975 production of Monteverdi's L'incoronazione di Poppea
(1642), shortly after its re-introduction to modern audiences.

1612, and in 1613 became *maestro di cappella* at St Mark's Cathedral in Venice, where he remained for the rest of his life. He also continued to write ballets and operas for the Mantuan court, but many of his scores were destroyed when Austrian troops sacked the palace in 1630. In the same year Venice was ravaged by plague, and shortly afterwards Monteverdi renounced the world and took holy orders.

In 1637, after the first public opera house opened in Venice, he was commissioned to write several operas. The two that survive – *Il ritorno d'Ulisse in patria* (*The Return of Ulysses*)

ABOVE: The sinfonia da guerra *(Battle Sinfonia) from the score of Monteverdi's* Il ritorno d'Ulisse in patria *(1640).*

and *L'incoronazione di Poppea* (*The Coronation of Poppea*) – are masterpieces of the genre in their superb characterization and instinctive feel for dramatic effect. The final scene of *L'incoronazione di Poppea*, despite celebrating the union of two ambitious and deeply unpleasant people, contains one of the most intensely passionate love duets in all opera.

The works of Monteverdi's Venetian years include three more madrigal collections. Book 8 of 1638, entitled *Madrigali guerrieri et amorosi* (*Songs of War and Love*), contains substantial dramatic works such as *Il ballo delle ingrate*, and the famous *Combattimento di Tancredi e Clorinda*, a graphic description of a duel between the Christian knight Tancred and the pagan Clorinda, who is disguised as a man. As a whole, the madrigal collections show Monteverdi moving with the times, from typically Renaissance polyphonic pieces in the earlier volumes (one of the most beautiful and frequently performed of these is the five-voice *Zefiro torna*, a setting of words by Petrarch), to highly expressive dramatic works for

solo voices with instrumental accompaniment in the later ones. All his music, early or late, is characterized by qualities of emotional intensity, depth of expression and understanding of human nature comparable with those that inform the works of Shakespeare.

ABOVE: The title page of a collection of poetical tributes in commemoration of Monteverdi's death, published in 1644.

Heinrich Schütz

The most spiritual musician the world has ever seen.

ALFRED EINSTEIN (1880–1952)

The achievements of J. S. Bach would not have been possible without the ground-breaking work of his illustrious predecessor, Heinrich Schütz. Born into a middle-class family of innkeepers in Saxony, Schütz became the most esteemed German composer of the 17th century. During two prolonged visits to Italy – the first, made while he was still a law student, enabling him to study in Venice with Giovanni Gabrieli – Schütz absorbed the Italian style, which he then amalgamated with the very different musical tradition of his native Germany.

Dresden *Kapellmeister*

On his return from Italy in 1613 after Gabrieli's death, Schütz became organist and then *Kapellmeister* at the electoral

ABOVE: *A portrait of Heinrich Schütz (1585–1672), by his contemporary Christoph Spetner.*

ABOVE: *Schütz's birthplace in Bad Köstritz, Germany. The building is now a museum devoted to the composer.*

court in Dresden, the most important musical centre in Protestant Germany. He published his first important compositions in 1619. These were a collection of settings for voices (some with instrumental interludes in the Venetian style) of the Psalms of David, described as "various motets and concertos". In the same year he married Magdalena Wildeck, daughter of a court official. Their happy union, which produced two daughters, was tragically brief: Magdalena died in 1625, and the grief-stricken composer never remarried. He outlived both his children: the elder died at the age of 16, and the younger in 1655, aged 31.

Schütz's court duties included writing music for official events, such as weddings and funerals. For the wedding of the elector's daughter to the Landgrave of Hessen-Darmstadt in 1627, he wrote the first German opera, setting the same libretto (*Dafne*) which the Italian composer Jacopo Peri had set 30 years earlier. Unfortunately the music has not survived.

In 1628 Schütz paid a second visit to Italy, where he met Monteverdi. This contact with recent musical developments bore fruit in a second published collection of vocal and instrumental music, *Symphoniae sacrae*. But there were troubles at home: Germany had entered the Thirty Years

War, and the Elector of Dresden found himself unable to pay his employees. Schütz escaped for two years to the court of the Crown Prince of Denmark, for whose wedding festivities he provided elaborate musical entertainments. But despite constant financial problems, he remained in the service of the Dresden court (apart from two more visits to Denmark) until 1657, when he was pensioned off. After his retirement he continued to write works for the electoral chapel until his death at the age of 87.

Schütz's music

Although Schütz was an enormously prolific composer, many of his manuscripts were destroyed by fire or the ravages of war. Even so, some 500 works survive. *Die Geburt unsers Herren Jesu Christi* (*The History of the Birth of Jesus Christ*), performed at Christmas Vespers at the Dresden court in 1660,

ABOVE: Gondolas moored near the Rialto Bridge in Venice, where Schütz studied with Giovanni Gabrieli.

is the earliest known German setting of the Nativity story in which the words of the Evangelist – or Narrator – are sung in recitative, rather than chanted as in earlier settings. His settings of the four Passions, together with innumerable psalm and motet settings and Italianate madrigals, influenced later composers such as Bach. Although Schütz's music fell out of fashion fairly rapidly, it was rediscovered in the 20th century, and championed by performers such as Roger Norrington in Britain, who founded first the amateur Heinrich Schütz Choir in 1962, and then the professional Schütz Choir of London.

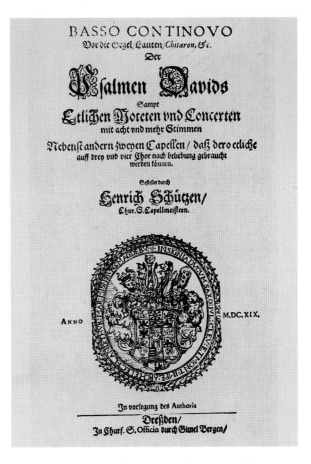

ABOVE: The title page of Schütz's Psalmen Davids, *settings of the Psalms for voices and instruments published in 1619.*

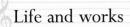
Life and works

NATIONALITY: German

BORN: Köstritz, 1585; DIED: Dresden, 1672

SPECIALIST GENRES: Sacred vocal and instrumental music, including oratorios and Passions.

MAJOR WORKS: *Psalmen Davids* (1619); *Cantiones sacrae* (1625); opera *Dafne* (1627); *Symphoniae sacrae* (1629, 1647, 1650); *Sieben Worte Jesu Christi am Kreuz* (*Seven Words of Christ on the Cross*, 1645); Christmas Oratorio (1660); Passions according to Matthew, Mark, Luke and John (1664–6).

Jean-Baptiste Lully

The musician is to follow the poet's direction, only in my opinion, Lully is to be exempted,
who knows the passions and enters further into the heart of man than the authors themselves.

SEIGNEUR DE SAINT-EVREMOND (1610–1703)

The founder of French opera owed his success partly to his exceptional talent, and partly to his ruthless, ambitious nature – only Wagner has rivalled Lully in sheer single-mindedness of purpose and grandiose vision. His career mirrored that of his patron, the "Sun King" Louis XIV (1643–1715), perhaps the greatest European monarch of his age, who saw his own glory reflected in the sumptuous entertainments devised by his clever court composer.

King and composer enjoyed a close, symbiotic relationship: indeed Lully's death, in 1687 at the age of only 55, marked the zenith of the Sun King's reign. Thereafter it was a long, slow story of royal decline, marked by personal misfortunes and military defeats.

ABOVE: Louis XIV's court composer, Jean-Baptiste Lully (1632–87).

The ambitious page

The son of a humble Florentine miller, Lully's singing voice was spotted at the age of 13 and he was taken to Paris and employed as a pageboy to a distant member of the royal family. Having perfected his own talents for dancing and playing the violin, he applied himself to social climbing, and quickly got his first royal appointment. His job was to write music for the lavish court ballets, and to drill the orchestra which accompanied them, the *Vingt-quatre violons du roi*. He soon established himself as a strict disciplinarian with a quick temper – later in life, as director of the opera house in Paris, he allegedly punched his pregnant leading lady in the stomach, causing her to miscarry, rather than jeopardize his productions.

ABOVE: The courtyard of Louis XIV's palace at Versailles, the envy of many other European monarchs. Many of Lully's court ballets and comedy-ballets were performed here.

ABOVE: A 17th-century engraving of Lully in his role as director of the royal orchestra.

ABOVE: An original stage design by Jean Berain for Lully's tragédie-lyrique, Armide, *first performed at the Académie Royale de Musique in Paris in 1686.*

Lully's ruthless nature suited his purposes well. He made an expedient marriage in order to disguise his homosexuality – a predilection which the king (a great lover of women) abhorred – and consolidated his position at court by choosing as his bride the daughter of the court composer, Michael Lambert. Meanwhile he cultivated the playwright Molière (1622–73), with whom he collaborated on several *comédies-ballets* (a hybrid form – half play, half ballet) for the entertainment of the court. The most famous of these was *Le bourgeois gentilhomme* (1670).

Opera at Versailles and Paris

Lully's next move, in 1672, was to take advantage of the bankruptcy of a fellow musician who had obtained a royal licence to import Italian opera. Lully seized the licence for himself, and while continuing to supply music for lavish court entertainments at the magnificent new palace of Versailles, he established a virtual monopoly over operatic productions, opening his own opera house in a disused tennis court

in Paris. The following year he turned his old friend Molière's troupe of actors out of their centrally sited theatre in the Palais Royal, and took it over, with the king's permission, rent-free.

Over the next 14 years, Lully and the poet Philippe Quinault (1635–88) produced a succession of brilliant operas in an entirely new and original style. These "lyric tragedies" were

ABOVE: A costume design for a character in Armide, *regarded as Lully's masterpiece.*

based on subjects drawn from mythology and legend (such as *Isis, Thésée, Phaëton* and *Armide*), worked into plots which subtly flattered Louis XIV – his victories, his devotion to duty and his personal concept of glory. Audiences of the time loved them – as did the king. Lully had struck gold, and made a huge fortune.

A bizarre end

Lully's court position required him to compose sacred music for the royal chapel, and while conducting a Te Deum written to celebrate Louis XIV's recovery from illness, he accidentally struck his foot with the heavy stick he used to mark the beat by banging it on the floor. Gangrene set in, but Lully refused to have the toe amputated.

As he lay dying, he was visited by a priest. In a final dramatic gesture to mark his penitence, Lully threw his last opera manuscript on to the fire, and received absolution. After the priest had gone, a horrified friend asked Lully why he had wantonly destroyed his last great work. "Don't worry," whispered the dying man, "I've got another copy!"

Arcangelo Corelli

I never met with any man that suffered his passions to hurry him away so much whilst he was playing on the violin as the famous Arcangelo Corelli, whose eyes will sometimes turn as red as fire.

FRANÇOIS RAGUENET (C.1660–1722)

While 17th-century German composers were bringing the art of organ-playing to a peak of perfection, Italy remained pre-eminent for nurturing the art of the violin. With the products of an unsurpassed school of instrument-makers – the Amati and Guarneri families, Stradivari, Gasparò da Salo and Maggini – at their disposal, Italian performers could hardly fail to establish a European reputation as masters of their art. One of the most influential of these – both in terms of violin technique and musical style – was Arcangelo Corelli.

Success as a performer

Corelli came from Fusignano, a town between Bologna and Ravenna. He took music lessons from a priest in nearby Faenza, and in 1666 arrived in Bologna, where he studied the violin

ABOVE: *Arcangelo Corelli, probably painted by the Flemish artist Jan Frans van Douven around 1700.*

with several fine players. By 1675 he had made his professional debut in Rome where, over the next few years, he established himself as a brilliant performer, taking part in the elaborate church performances commissioned by Rome's decadent but artistically inclined prelates, and in secular performances at the theatres. In 1679 he became chamber musician to the exiled Queen Christina of Sweden, to whom he dedicated his first compositions, a set of 12 *sonate da chiesa*.

Before long, the ambitious violinist had decided to replace his patron with a more influential one: Cardinal Pamphili, one of the richest men in Rome. From 1684 onwards Corelli began to play regularly at musical events organized by Pamphili, while introducing his own works – including a set of chamber trios

LEFT: *A highly romanticized impression (1913) of the violin maker Antonio Stradivari in his workshop at Cremona, by Edgar Bundy (1862–1922).*

RIGHT:
The Hellier *Stradivarius, made in 1679.*

ABOVE: *The title page of Corelli's Op. 1 trio sonatas, published in 1685 with a dedication to Queen Christina of Sweden.*

dedicated to Pamphili – at the musical academies held on Sunday afternoons at the cardinal's sumptuous palazzo. His social climbing bore fruit, and in July 1687 he was formally engaged as the cardinal's music master, and given a suite of rooms in the palace.

Orchestral compositions

In 1690 Pamphili moved to Bologna, but Corelli declined to follow him. Instead, he was engaged by a rival cardinal, the young Pietro Ottoboni, nephew of Pope Alexander VIII, another ostentatious patron of the arts. Corelli and Ottoboni became good friends, and Corelli dedicated a second set of chamber trios to him in 1694. He also began to write orchestral works (sinfonias and concertos), which attracted much attention. He was described as "the famous violinist...the Orpheus of our time," whose works were "prized and esteemed".

In 1702, however, his self-esteem was shaken when he visited Naples to play in the opera orchestra, taking with him two Roman players since he distrusted the abilities of the Neapolitans. To his surprise, he found that the despised southerners could actually play quite well, while he himself had embarrassing difficulty with a particular passage that his hosts managed fluently.

In 1707 Corelli met Handel (who was working in Rome), and played in a performance of an early Handel oratorio. Shortly afterwards he retired from playing to devote himself to composition. His health deteriorated, and he died early in 1713. He was buried in the Pantheon. His reputation both as performer and composer long outlived him: his compositions were reprinted many times and sold all over Europe. They were particularly popular in England and Germany, where they influenced many later composers, including Handel, Telemann and Bach.

ABOVE: *Queen Christina holding court. She is talking with the French philosopher René Descartes (painting by Dumesnil the Younger, 1698–1781).*

Henry Purcell

*Mr Purcell, in whose person we have at length found
an Englishman equal with the best abroad.*

JOHN DRYDEN (1631–1700)

Unlike some European countries, which enjoyed a strong and continuing musical tradition from the Renaissance onwards, England – while strong on literature – has suffered from a distinctly patchy musical heritage. After the Elizabethan flowering, only a few distinctive figures emerged in the early 17th century – notably the Lawes brothers, Henry (1596–1662) and William (1602–45), and later John Blow (1649–1708); but England produced no composer of European stature until the brilliant but tragically short-lived Henry Purcell.

Occasional music

Purcell began his career as a chorister in the Chapel Royal; in 1679 he succeeded Blow as organist of Westminster Abbey. He seems to have married around 1680, and had several children, of whom a son and a daughter survived him. In 1682 he was appointed an organist of the Chapel Royal, and a year later became organ-maker and keeper of the king's instruments.

His court appointments were renewed after Charles II's death, and he continued to produce many odes and welcome songs (cantata-like compositions) for occasions such as royal birthdays, marriages and New Year's Day. Most of these "occasional" works are now among the least known of his output, but the 1692 Ode for St Cecilia's Day, *Hail, Bright Cecilia*, is one of his best-loved works.

*ABOVE:
A 19th-century
lithograph of
Henry Purcell by
Alfred Lemoine
(1824–81).*

*LEFT: William III
(1650–1702)
and his wife
Mary II (1662–
94), who reigned
jointly as King
and Queen of
England from
1689.*

Life and works

NATIONALITY: English

BORN: London, 1659;
DIED: London, 1695

SPECIALIST GENRES: Opera and incidental music for the stage, odes, anthems, instrumental music.

MAJOR WORKS: *Dido and Aeneas* (1689); *King Arthur* (1691); *The Fairy Queen* (1692); *Hail, Bright Cecilia* (1692); *Come, Ye Sons of Art* (1694); Te Deum and Jubilate in D (1694); Funeral music for Queen Mary (1695).

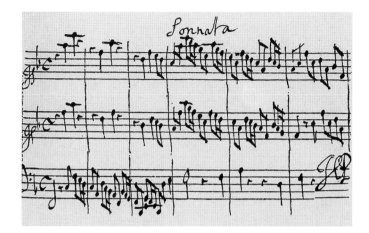

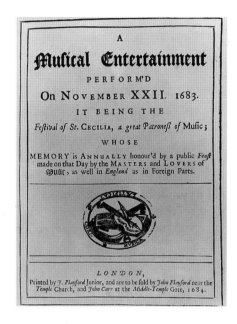

LEFT: *The opening of Purcell's* Golden Sonata *for two violins and* basso continuo.

RIGHT: *The frontispiece to the text of Purcell's 1683* Ode to St Cecilia, Welcome to all the pleasures.

Stage works

During the last decade of his life, Purcell combined his court duties with writing music for the stage. Opera as such did not exist in England at the time, but between 1690 and 1695 Purcell provided incidental music for five major "semi-operas" put on at London theatres: Betterton's *Dioclesian, King Arthur* and *The Indian Queen* (with texts by John Dryden), *The Fairy Queen* and *The Tempest* (both loosely based on Shakespeare).

Purcell's most famous stage work, however, is the opera *Dido and Aeneas*, long thought to have been written around 1689 for a girls' school in Chelsea, but possibly dating from several years earlier. He also provided individual musical items for over 40 other plays by the most notable playwrights of the time. The Rondeau from his music for Aphra Behn's 1695 play *Abdelazer* was used by Benjamin Britten as the theme of his *Young Person's Guide to the Orchestra* (1946).

Purcell's legacy

Apart from his dramatic music, Purcell wrote many exquisite anthems, a Magnificat and a Te Deum, a vast number of solo songs and partsongs (some with extremely bawdy texts which have only recently been permitted to surface), instrumental music including fantasias for viol consort, a set of 12 trio sonatas for two violins and continuo, a set of 10 sonatas "in four parts", clearly influenced by Corelli, and some charming keyboard music, including eight suites. Among his last works was the moving Funeral Music for Queen Mary, written for the young and much-mourned queen: within a short while Purcell had followed her to the grave at the age of only 36. The music he had written for the queen was played at his own funeral.

Purcell's genius lay in his unique response to the setting of English words, whether sacred or secular, his gift for appealing melody, his assimilation of elements from both Italian and French music – notably Corelli's violin writing, and Lully's unusual effects (the "Frost Scene" from *King Arthur*, in which each note is sung with a shiver, was borrowed from a similar scene in Lully's opera *Isis*) – and his forward-looking treatment of the orchestra, particularly the strings.

Though regarded as a "one-off" genius, the end of a tradition rather than an initiator, Purcell is still held in high esteem. *Dido and Aeneas* is often performed, and in the last decade of the 20th century, particularly during the tercentenary celebration of his death, most of his music was made widely available through high-quality performances and recordings.

ABOVE: *The choir of Westminster Abbey, where Purcell was buried at the foot of the organ.*

Antonio Vivaldi

He is an old man, who has a prodigious fury for composition. I heard him undertake to compose a concerto, with all the parts, with greater despatch than a copyist can copy it.

CHARLES DE BROSSES, 1739

For many people, the name Vivaldi is associated with just one piece of music – *Le quattro stagioni* (*The Four Seasons*) – which has been recorded countless times. But many other gems of Vivaldi's output are worth exploring: he was one of the most prolific and influential composers of his time, and without his contribution to the development of concerto form, the instrumental music of later composers such as Bach would have been the poorer.

The Red Priest
Vivaldi was born (during a minor earthquake) in Venice, to a baker turned professional violinist,

ABOVE: The violinist and composer Antonio Vivaldi (1678–1741), painted in 1723 by François Morellon La Cave.

with whom the young Antonio studied. In 1693 he began to train for the priesthood, while still living at home and continuing his violin studies. He was ordained in 1703, and his startling red hair earned him the nickname of *il prete rosso* (the Red Priest), but the ecclesiastical life did not entirely suit him, and several times he found himself at odds with the church authorities.

In the year of his ordination, Vivaldi was appointed violin teacher at the Conservatorio dell'Ospedale della Pietà, a Venetian orphanage which housed and educated young girls. Music was held in high esteem there,

and its reputation was such that many leading performers took part in its concerts. Vivaldi was required to teach and rehearse the students and to maintain the instruments. His initial appointment lasted six years, during which time he published a set of 12 trio *sonate da camera* and a set of solo violin sonatas. He had already begun to write concertos, which became his favourite medium.

Vivaldi's concertos
In all Vivaldi wrote well over 200 violin concertos, around 27 cello concertos, around a dozen for flute, three for

ABOVE: Vivaldi's family home on the Fondamenta del Dose in Venice.

ABOVE: A page from the cello part of Vivaldi's collection of concertos L'estro armonico.

piccolo, 20 for oboe, 37 for bassoon (an instrument for which few other composers have written concertos), and many more double and multiple concertos, of which the E minor concerto for four violins, Op. 3 No. 4, is very well known.

The fanciful titles of some of his concertos gave Vivaldi plenty of opportunity for descriptive writing. As well as the famous *Four Seasons*, programmatically depicting seasonal activities such as skating on the ice (winter), hunting (autumn), and listening to birdsong (spring), their titles include *La tempestà di mare* (*Storm at Sea*), *L'amoroso* (*The Lover*), *La caccia* (*The Hunt*) and *Il corneto di posta* (*The Posthorn*).

A set of 12 concertos for one, two or four solo violins was published in Amsterdam in 1711 under the title *L'estro armonico*, and instantly sold all over Europe (Bach made keyboard transcriptions of five of them). Another set of 12 (*La stravaganza*) appeared in 1714, and from then on Vivaldi's music was much in demand (the collection

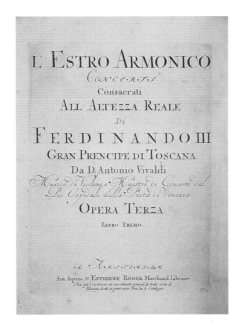

ABOVE: *The title page of Vivaldi's* L'estro armonico, *published 1711 with a dedication to the Grand Duke of Tuscany.*

containing *The Four Seasons* was published in 1725). He also wrote around 60 *concerti grossi* for strings and bass.

In 1711 Vivaldi returned to the Pietà, where he took the opportunity to write sacred as well as instrumental music. His cheerful *Gloria* is still much

performed today. He was associated with the institution until his death, although his frequent absences were not popular. He also began to write operas (about 45 in all) for various Italian courts and opera houses, including Mantua, Venice and Rome. Several have recently been revived, although interest still tends to be academic.

Fall from grace

Vivaldi spent much of the last two decades of his life on the move. Around 1725 he became involved with his singing pupil, Anna Giraud. The church authorities cannot have been pleased with the whiff of scandal surrounding the "Red Priest" and in 1737 he was censured for unpriestly conduct. In 1741 Vivaldi undertook a mysterious journey to Vienna (perhaps connected with Anna's work as an opera singer). He arrived on 28 June, and a month later he was dead, apparently of unknown causes. His arrogance and egotism had made many enemies, but his posthumous influence was immense.

Life and works

NATIONALITY: Italian

BORN: Venice, 1678;
DIED: Vienna, 1741

SPECIALIST GENRES: Instrumental music, especially violin concertos.

MAJOR WORKS: Over 400 concertos published in sets, including *L'estro armonico* (1711); *Il cimento dell'armonia e dell'inventione* (1725 – 12 concertos of which the first four are *Le quattro stagioni*).

ABOVE: *The Piazza San Marco in Venice, painted in 1723 during Vivaldi's lifetime by the Italian artist Canaletto.*

Johann Pachelbel

A perfect and rare virtuoso.

DANIEL EBERLIN (1647–C.1715)

Johann Pachelbel, an important predecessor of J. S. Bach, is remembered today chiefly for a single composition, known as "Pachelbel's Canon" (of which many versions – including rock – now exist). But in his day he was much admired for his contribution to German Protestant church music, particularly for the organ.

Born in Nuremberg, he began his career as organist at St Stephen's Cathedral in Vienna. In 1677 he became organist at Bach's birthplace, the Thuringian town of Eisenach, but a year later he moved a few miles east to Erfurt,

ABOVE: The title page of Pachelbel's Hexachordum Apollinis, *printed in Nuremberg in 1699, six "arias" for organ or harpsichord, with variations.*

where for the next 12 years he was organist at the Predigerkirche. There he came into contact with members of the Bach family (he was godfather to one of J. S. Bach's sisters, and taught his elder brother Johann Christoph, who in turn taught Johann Sebastian).

While at Erfurt, Pachelbel married, only to lose his wife and their baby son two years later in a plague epidemic. He remarried in 1684, and raised a family of seven children. He then spent two years as court organist at Stuttgart, and three as town organist at Gotha, before finally moving back to his own birthplace as organist of St Sebald's Church.

Pachelbel's music

The organ chorales composed by Pachelbel – complex polyphonic pieces based on Protestant hymn tunes – had

enormous influence on those of Bach. He was also a master of various other keyboard genres of the time, including toccatas, *ricercari*, fantasias, chaconnes and variations – his *Hexachordum Apollinis* (1699) is a group of six arias with variations for organ or harpsichord, each in one of five keys making up a perfect fifth.

Pachelbel also wrote six suites for two violins and keyboard, the masterly and justly famous Canon (a set of 28 canonic variations originally scored for three violins and bass), motets, sacred concertos and 11 fine settings of the Magnificat for chorus and instruments, intended for the Vesper services in Nuremberg.

ABOVE: A 1732 engraving of a concert with organ, strings, wind and brass instruments. Pachelbel specialized in organ church music.

Dietrich Buxtehude

I should place an organist who is master of his instrument
at the very head of all virtuosi.

LUDWIG VAN BEETHOVEN (1770–1827)

The Danish organist and composer Dietrich Buxtehude was an almost exact contemporary of Pachelbel, and like him, proved a formative influence on J. S. Bach. Probably of German origin, he was born some time around 1637 in the duchy of Holstein, where his father was a school-master and organist. In 1668 Buxtehude himself became organist at St Mary's Church in Lübeck, in north Germany. This appointment was one of the most important and lucrative in Germany, and competition was fierce (even though one of the stranger conditions attached to it was that the successful

ABOVE: A painting by Johannes Voorhout depicting the friendship between Dietrich Buxtehude and his colleague J. A. Reincken (at the harpsichord).

candidate should marry a daughter of his predecessor). This Buxtehude did – although Handel apparently declined an offer of the post nearly 40 years later when confronted with the necessity of marrying Buxtehude's own ageing daughter.

Buxtehude remained at Lübeck for the rest of his life. His duties at St Mary's required him to play and compose music for the main services, but he also reinstated an old tradition of giving substantial concerts in the church on the five Sundays before Christmas, just after the afternoon service. These *Abendmusiken*, as they were called, became famous, as was Buxtehude's extraordinarily accomplished organ-playing. In the winter of 1705–6, the young J. S. Bach is reputed to have walked from Thuringia to Lübeck just to hear the great man play.

ABOVE: St Mary's Church in Lübeck, where Buxtehude was organist for nearly 40 years, and where Bach heard him play.

Buxtehude's music

Buxtehude left a substantial body of compositions, including cantatas, several oratorio-like works intended for the *Abendmusiken*, many organ works including chorale preludes, fantasias, fugues and variations based on chorale themes, as well as some lighter chamber and keyboard music. His organ works, which had enormous influence on Bach, exploit the characteristic range of tone-colour of north German organs of the period, and liberate the pedal from its traditional role as harmonic foundation – some of Buxtehude's pedal parts require virtuoso footwork in their own right.

Life and works

NATIONALITY: Danish

BORN: Oldesloe, c.1637; **DIED:** Lübeck, 1707

SPECIALIST GENRES: Organ music, cantatas for the German Protestant liturgy.

MAJOR WORKS: 120 sacred cantatas and other vocal pieces; many organ works; chamber and keyboard music.

Johann Sebastian Bach

Johann Sebastian Bach has done everything completely,
he was a man through and through.

Franz Schubert (1797–1828)

For many music-lovers, the music of J. S. Bach fulfils a profound spiritual need: it has a timeless, other-worldly quality which could only come from a composer who felt himself close to God. Just as Bach's birthplace was over-shadowed by the Wartburg mountain, topped by the fortress in which Martin Luther hammered out the fundamental principles of Protestant theology, so his life was dominated by his devotion to the Lutheran faith, and his music was dedicated to its service.

Early years

Unlike many of his more cosmopolitan contemporaries, Bach spent his entire career in Germany – mostly in the central regions of Thuringia and Saxony. He was born into a long dynasty of Thuringian organists and composers who worked as church organists and choir-masters, municipal musicians, and at the many small princely or ducal courts which flourished in the region. Bach's father, Ambrosius, was himself employed as a musician by the town council of Eisenach, where Johann Sebastian was born on 21 March 1685.

After losing both parents by the age of ten, Bach was sent to live at Ohrdruf with his married elder brother, Johann Christoph, who was organist there. It seems likely that Johann Christoph helped with his young brother's musical training, but once Johann Sebastian reached the age of 15, there was no longer room for him in the Ohrdruf household, and he obtained a free place at St Michael's

ABOVE: The house where Bach is believed to have been born in the Rittergasse in Eisenach, Thuringia, now a Bach museum.

ABOVE: Johann Sebastian Bach, four years before his death, in a painting by E. G. Haussmann.

RIGHT:
A room in Bach's probable birthplace, containing contemporary instruments.

LEFT: *A view of Eisenach, with the Wartburg Castle on the hill behind.*

RIGHT: *Thomaskirche in Leipzig, where Bach was an organist and choir-master, and where he was subsequently interred.*

School in Lüneburg, 320km (200 miles) away in north Germany. There he benefited from a solid musical education and sang in the choir, but his formal education came to an end in 1702.

Arnstadt and Mühlhausen

At the age of 17, Bach returned to his native Thuringia to look for a job. After a temporary spell as a violinist at the Weimar ducal court, he was appointed organist at the New Church in Arnstadt, not far from Weimar. There he started to compose in earnest, and in the winter of 1705–6 he made his legendary pilgrimage (allegedly on foot) to Lübeck, 420km (260 miles) to the north, to hear the celebrated organist Dietrich Buxtehude.

After his return to Arnstadt, Bach's relationship with the church council deteriorated (he had a stubborn and at times arrogant streak, which caused problems with all his employers), and in the summer of 1707 he left to take up a new post as organist at the imperial free city of Mühlhausen, some 58km (36 miles) to the north-west. His salary was now such that he felt able to marry his second cousin, Maria Barbara Bach. But although his personal life had settled down, Bach quickly became dissatisfied with conditions at Mühlhausen, and in 1708 he moved again, this time to the ducal court at Weimar.

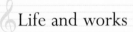

ABOVE: *Bach directing a concert in 1714 at the Court Chapel in Weimar, where he worked from 1708 until 1717.*

Weimar

In the early 18th century Weimar was just another small, provincial town – its period of glory was to come some 80 years later, when its residents would include Goethe, Wieland and Schiller. Bach's job was as organist at the ducal chapel in the castle, but six of his children – including the future composers Wilhelm Friedemann (1710–84) and Carl Philipp Emmanuel (1714–88) – were christened at the City Church of St Peter and Paul during the Weimar years.

It was here that Bach began composing cantatas in earnest for performance at court, and he also provided instrumental music for the court orchestra. His early years at Weimar were happy and productive but, after 1713, relations with his employer, Duke Wilhelm Ernst, began to deteriorate and in 1717 Bach accepted

ABOVE: A romanticized artist's impression of Bach's visit to Frederick the Great at the palace of Sans Souci in Potsdam, May 1747.

the job of *Kapellmeister* to the court of Prince Leopold of Anhalt-Cöthen. The duke was so reluctant to let him go that he placed him under house arrest for a month. Eventually, in December 1717, the Bach family was allowed to leave.

Cöthen

While most of Bach's compositions up to 1717 had been organ works and sacred cantatas, he now exploited the instrumental resources available to him at the Cöthen court. Most of his work there was secular, since the Calvinist Prince Leopold required little sacred music. Among the works he composed during this period were the six *Brandenburg Concertos* for various instrumental combinations, together

with concertos for violin (including the famous Double Concerto in D minor), orchestral suites, sonatas for harpsichord, violin, and flute, the suites for solo cello and the sonatas and partitas for solo violin. These works show that Bach had thoroughly absorbed the Italian style, through intensive study of works by Corelli and Vivaldi.

Remarriage

In May 1720, while Bach was away at a spa with his employer, Maria Barbara died suddenly. Bach remarried the next year: his bride, Anna Magdalena Wilcken (1701–60), proved a great asset to her husband, both domestically and professionally (the daughter of a musician, she was a singer, harpsichordist and music copyist). She inherited Bach's four surviving

ABOVE: Bach's eldest son, Wilhelm Friedemann (1710–84), painted around 1760. Like his father, he was a composer.

ABOVE: The trumpeter Gottfried Reiche (1667–1734), who played the high clarino parts in Bach's works in Leipzig.

children, to whom she added another 13, including another future composer, Johann Christian (1735–82), later known as the "English Bach", since he spent much of his career there. Shortly after their marriage Bach began to compile two *Clavierbüchlein* (*Little Keyboard Books*) for his wife, which contain, among other works, the 15 Inventions and Sinfonias and several preludes and fugues, which were later assembled with others as *Das wohltemperierte Clavier* (*The Well-Tempered Clavier*).

In 1721 Prince Leopold of Anhalt-Cöthen married his cousin, and life changed irrevocably at the Cöthen court. The frivolous new princess was uninterested in music, and Bach soon felt obliged to move on – probably with some regret. In June 1722 the post of Kantor of the Thomasschule in Leipzig became vacant. The town council wanted Telemann, but he could not be released from his job at Hamburg, and so, after much deliberation, they appointed Bach. On 22 May 1723 he moved into his new quarters in the Thomasschule, where he stayed until his death 27 years later.

Leipzig

Bach's years at Leipzig, where he was required not only to teach, but to supply music for the town's two principal churches, St Thomas and St Nicholas, were relatively uneventful, but were punctuated by acrimonious disagreements with the council over pay and conditions. Nonetheless, they were amazingly fruitful. One of his principal jobs was to write, rehearse and direct cantatas for the Sunday services at the two churches, and his output included around 250 of these substantial works for voices, chorus

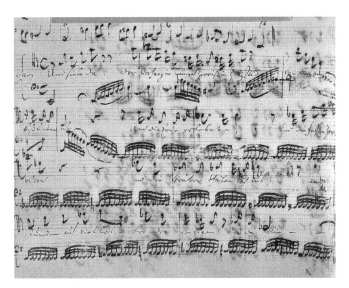

ABOVE: A page from the manuscript score of Bach's St Matthew Passion, *first performed in Leipzig on Good Friday in 1729.*

and orchestra, mostly based on well-known Protestant chorale tunes.

In addition, he produced two magnificent settings of the Passion story, according to St Matthew and St John, the Mass in B minor, the *Christmas Oratorio*, and other major sacred works, into which he poured all the resources of vocal and instrumental writing available to him. Towards the end of his life, several books of keyboard music were published, but Bach's fame remained local. Among his last major

works were the *Goldberg Variations* for harpsichord, allegedly written for an aristocratic insomniac; *Das musicalisches Opfer* (*The Musical Offering*, based on a fugue subject devised by Frederick the Great when Bach visited him at Potsdam in 1747), and the almost visionary *Kunst der Fuge* (*The Art of Fugue*), a complex series of canons on which Bach worked during the last years of his life, when his sight began to fail. He was almost totally blind when he died, leaving his widow in dire financial straits.

By the time of Bach's death, musical fashions were fast changing, and his music was perceived as antiquated. During his lifetime he had been more celebrated as an organist than as a composer. Unlike Mozart or Beethoven, he had little posthumous influence until Mendelssohn rediscovered his choral masterpieces in the 19th century, and his works began to be performed once more. He is now revered as one of the greatest of all composers.

ABOVE: A romanticized 19th-century impression of the Bach family at their morning prayers.

George Frideric Handel

Handel understands effect better than any of us —
when he chooses, he strikes like a thunderbolt.

WOLFGANG AMADEUS MOZART (1756–91)

Handel and Bach were born in the same year, in much the same area of central Germany – Halle, Handel's birthplace in Saxony, is about 160km (100 miles) north of Thuringia. Both men lived to a reasonable old age, and both had lost their sight when they died. But their respective careers could not have been more different.

Early years

While Bach was content to live and work within the musical tradition of his family, Handel had to struggle to make a career in music. His father wanted his son to study law, and tried to stifle the boy's interest in music. But Handel persisted, and was eventually allowed to study music as part of his general education. Only after his father's death did he take it up full-time and in 1703, aged 18, he set out for Hamburg in search of employment.

ABOVE: George Frideric Handel (1685–1759). He never appeared in public without his voluminous wig.

Hamburg

One of Hamburg's attractions was as a flourishing centre of opera. Germany's first commercial opera house had opened there in 1678, and had scraped along financially under a succession of entrepreneurial directors with flair but no money. Here Handel found an ideal proving-ground for his early attempts at the genre which would dominate his life. But he refused the offer of a permanent post, and instead departed for Italy – the birthplace of opera.

The Italian experience

Handel travelled to Italy under the patronage of Prince Ferdinando de'Medici, and in 1707 his first mature opera, *Rodrigo*, was produced at a Florentine theatre. It was a success, earning Handel the favours of the grand duke's mistress, the singer Vittoria Tarquini. Perhaps wisely, Handel quickly departed for Rome, where he found employment at the court of Cardinal Pietro Ottoboni, the immensely wealthy papal vice-chancellor. There he met celebrated musicians including Corelli and the Scarlattis, and tried his hand at music for the unfamiliar Catholic liturgy, including a setting of the Vespers. His first oratorio, a setting of the Resurrection story, was performed with great splendour on Easter Sunday 1708 at the Palazzo Bonelli.

From Rome Handel travelled on to Naples and then to Venice, where his opera *Agrippina* was performed during

ABOVE: An anonymous painting of Hamburg, one of the most important of the Hanseatic ports, in 1700.

ABOVE: *The square in front of St Peter's Basilica in Rome, painted in 1754 by G. P. Pannini.*

ABOVE: *A romantic impression depicting Handel making music at the keyboard with his friends.*

the 1710 carnival season. Then, ever eager for new experiences, he returned north to Hanover, to be appointed *Kapellmeister* to the elector at a good salary and with the promise of a year's sabbatical leave. He took it immediately, and promptly left with an invitation to London. His transformation from a German to an English composer had begun.

England

In Queen Anne's England, Handel stepped into a musical vacuum left by the deaths of John Blow and his gifted pupil Henry Purcell. He decided to fill it by satisfying the growing middle-class demand for opera. His opera *Rinaldo* scored a huge success at the Queen's Theatre in London, both musically and dramatically. Audiences were particularly intrigued by a dramatic masterstroke – the release of a flock of sparrows onstage to lend verisimilitude to the aria "Augelletti" ("Little Birds"). But Handel was under an obligation to return to Hanover, where he spent some 15 months

perfecting his instrumental compositions – overtures and *concerti grossi*.

In the autumn of 1712 Handel obtained another period of leave from the indulgent Elector of Hanover, and

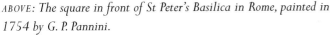

Life and works

NATIONALITY: German

BORN: Halle, 1685;
DIED: London, 1759

SPECIALIST GENRES:
Italianate operas,
English oratorios.

MAJOR WORKS:
Water Music (1717);
Acis and Galatea (1718) and
45 other operas; *Chandos
Anthems* (1717–20);
12 *concerti grossi* (1739);
Messiah (1742); 15 other
oratorios; *Music for the
Royal Fireworks* (1749).

returned to London, where his next opera, *Il pastor fido* (*The Faithful Shepherd*), was put on at the Haymarket Theatre. This time the public was disappointed. As one critic put it: "The habits [costumes] were old. The opera short." Handel immediately hit back with a full-length, five-act opera, based on the Greek myth of Theseus. At the same time he began to fulfil royal commissions, supplying royal odes and a triumphantly received Te Deum and Jubilate to celebrate the Treaty of Utrecht, which ended the War of the Spanish Succession.

Life under a new king

Handel had absented himself from his duties in Hanover for two years when in 1714 he received a rude shock: Queen Anne died childless, and the English throne passed to his neglected former employer the Elector of Hanover, now George I of England. It is said that the famous *Water Music*, written to accompany the king's triumphal procession up the Thames, was composed as a peace-offering (although it was probably written three

ABOVE: *Handel playing one of his organ concertos at the Covent Garden Theatre in London.*

Radamisto, Rodelinda, Admeto, Giulio Cesare and Tamerlano, and engaged some of the finest European singers to perform them. These included the great castrato Senesino, a man possessed of a "powerful, clear, equal and sweet contralto voice", and the sopranos Francesca Cuzzoni and Faustina Bordoni, all engaged at astronomical salaries. Apart from the entertainment of the operas themselves, London society was soon treated to the diverting spectacle of the two rival divas fighting on stage while Senesino spent his time sulking in the background.

Change to oratorio

George I died in 1727. For his successor, George II's, coronation Handel provided four anthems (including *Zadok the Priest*, which has been sung at British coronations ever since). By this time the Academy was in deep financial trouble, and Handel's own financial losses – combined with waning public enthusiasm for this "exotic and irrational entertainment", the unexpected popularity of John Gay's satirical *Beggar's Opera* in 1728, and a complete breakdown in health – prompted a change of direction. He was already

years after George's accession). In any case, Handel was quickly forgiven, and remained a favoured royal composer for the rest of his life. He also acquired a new patron, the Duke of Chandos, for whose magnificent estate in Edgware Handel wrote the 11 *Chandos Anthems*, a Te Deum, the masque *Acis and Galatea*, and his first attempt at an English oratorio, *Esther*.

The Royal Academy

In 1719 the grandly named Royal Academy of Music came into being. This institution, supported by a group of 62 royal and noble subscribers, aimed to establish a regular opera company in London, with Handel as its composer-in-residence. Over the next eight years he supplied some 14 Italian operas for the company, including

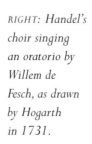

LEFT: *The aria "How beautiful are the feet" from Handel's autograph score of* Messiah.

RIGHT: *Handel's choir singing an oratorio by Willem de Fesch, as drawn by Hogarth in 1731.*

writing instrumental music, especially organ concertos, for the London pleasure gardens, but although he continued to write Italian operas, including *Ariodante* and *Serse*, until 1740, he needed a new genre. He found it in the English oratorio, beginning with *Deborah*, *Athaliah*, *Saul* and *Israel in Egypt* in the 1730s, but reaching its apogee in *Messiah*, written for performance in Dublin in 1742.

In setting these Biblical stories, Handel adapted elements from Italian opera, particularly the recitative-aria format; but reduced the soloists' importance in order to give more prominence to the chorus and orchestra. This clever ploy ensured the survival of his oratorios as a mainstay of the repertoire of British choral societies. *Messiah* was followed by some 15 further oratorios, including *Samson* (1741–2), *Semele* (1743), which is more of an opera than an oratorio, *Judas Maccabaeus* (1746), *Alexander Balue* and *Joshua* (1747), *Solomon* (1748) and *Jephtha* (1751), all of which are still regularly performed.

ABOVE: *Handel's memorial in Westminster Abbey, London.*

Last years

Handel's fortunes were mixed in the last years of his life. He had amassed considerable wealth despite his losses, and used some of it to support philanthropic causes, such as the Foundling Hospital. In April 1749 he fulfilled his last royal commission:

music to accompany a grand firework display in London's Green Park to mark the Peace of Aix-la-Chapelle – an occasion marred when the firework pavilion burnt to the ground. But Handel's *Music for the Royal Fireworks* ranks with the *Water Music* among his most popular instrumental compositions.

Two years later his sight was failing. A painful operation to cure cataracts proved useless, and for the last seven years of his life he was totally blind. But the people of his adopted land had taken him to their hearts, and while Bach's death went largely unremarked, Handel was buried with full honours in Westminster Abbey. His epitaph summed up his extraordinary achievement:

The most Excellent Musician any Age ever produced: Whose Compositions were a Sentimental Language rather than mere Sounds; And surpassed the Power of Words In Expressing the various Passions of the Human Heart.

ABOVE: *A contemporary artist's view of the structure erected in Green Park for the 1749 firework display celebrating the Peace of Aix-la-Chapelle.*

ABOVE: *The Handel Centenary Commemoration concert (1785) in Westminster Abbey.*

Domenico Scarlatti

*Scarlatti frequently told M. L'Augier that he was sensible
he had broke through all the rules of composition…*

CHARLES BURNEY (1726–1814), "GENERAL HISTORY OF MUSIC"

The son of the composer Alessandro Scarlatti, Domenico probably began his musical training with his father. At the age of 16 he was appointed organist in the Neapolitan royal chapel, where his father was *maestro di cappella,* but in the spring of 1705 Alessandro ordered his son to seek his fortune in the northern Italian cities of Florence and Venice, describing him in a letter of recommendation as "a young eagle whose wings are grown: he must not remain idle in the nest, and I must not hinder his flight". In fact, Alessandro continued to interfere with his son's career until Domenico obtained legal independence in 1717, at the advanced age of 32.

In 1709 Domenico entered the service of the exiled Polish Queen Maria Casimira in Rome, where he encountered other up-and-coming musicians, including his contemporary,

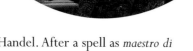

Handel. After a spell as *maestro di cappella* at the Julian Chapel in the Vatican, he decided to leave Italy for Portugal, and from 1719 until 1728 he worked in Lisbon.

Keyboard sonatas

Scarlatti's duties in Lisbon included teaching the king's musical daughter Maria Barbara. When the princess married the Crown Prince of Spain and moved to Madrid in 1728, Scarlatti accompanied her. He remained in her service for the rest of his life, and it was for her that he wrote the 550 or so one-movement keyboard sonatas on which his fame rests.

These sonatas are unique in the keyboard repertoire. Apart from their unusual binary format, they explore new playing techniques, including hand-crossing and rapid note repetition. Each sonata, which Scarlatti himself described as "an ingenious jesting with art", focuses on a particular technical problem, and many incorporate special effects in imitation of Spanish idioms, such as the thrumming of guitars and the clicking of castanets.

*ABOVE:
A contemporary portrait in oil of Domenico Scarlatti by Antonio de Velasco.*

LEFT: The Harpsichordist, *by Edith Hipkins (1885), now in the Royal Academy of Music in London.*

Life and works

NATIONALITY: Italian

BORN: Naples, 1685;
DIED: Madrid, 1757

SPECIALIST GENRES:
Virtuoso harpsichord music.

MAJOR WORKS:
550 keyboard sonatas.

Jean-Philippe Rameau

The expression of thought, of sentiment, of the passions,
must be the true aim of music.

RAMEAU

The French composer Jean-Philippe Rameau is now chiefly remembered for his operas, but like Janáček, he was a late starter in the operatic field. Born two years before the great Bach-Handel-Scarlatti triumvirate, he spent the earlier part of his career working as an organist, moving between various major towns in central France and Paris, where he eventually settled in 1722. In that year he published a textbook on harmony, *Traité de l'harmonie,* which established him as one of the most innovative and controversial musical theorists of his age.

Over the next 25 years or so Rameau worked principally as a harpsichord teacher, and his volumes of enchanting "character" pieces for keyboard in the tradition of François Couperin became very popular. In 1730 he found a wealthy patron, the tax-collector Le Riche de

ABOVE: *Jean-Philippe Rameau with his violin, a famous portrait by Joseph Aved (1702–66).*

la Pouplinière, who introduced him to the playwright Abbé Simon-Joseph Pellegrin. Rameau's first opera, *Hippolyte et Aricie,* to a libretto by Pellegrin, was produced at the Paris Opéra in October 1733. It established the composer as a worthy successor to Lully in the operatic field.

Rameau went on to write some 30 stage works – full-blown *tragédies-lyriques* in the Lullian mould such as *Castor et Pollux, Dardanus* and *Les boréades;* opera-ballets (operas with a substantial dance element, often written to celebrate royal victories or marriages), such as *La princesse de Navarre, Les fêtes de Polymnie* and *Zaïs;* and straightforward ballets such as *Pygmalion.* All are characterized by

sensitive handling of the text, whether comic, sentimental or tragic; colourful and innovative use of the orchestra (especially evident in the many brilliant and lively dances); and expressive and powerful choral writing.

War of the Buffoons

In the early 1750s Rameau (or rather his supporters) became embroiled in the celebrated *"Querelle des bouffons"* – a war of words between admirers of Rameau's traditional French style, and those of the newly imported Italian style of Pergolesi. In the long run, the Italians won, and Rameau's operas finally dropped out of fashion. They were resurrected some 200 years later by William Christie's *Les arts florissants* in France and the British conductors John Eliot Gardiner and Nicholas Kraemer.

ABOVE: *Sophie Arnould (1740–1802), one of the most celebrated French opera singers of Rameau's time.*

Life and works

NATIONALITY: French

BORN: Dijon, 1683;
DIED: Paris, 1764

SPECIALIST GENRES: Opera and opera-ballets in the French style.

MAJOR WORKS: *Les Indes galantes* (*The Courtly Indies,* 1735); *Castor et Pollux* (1737); *Pièces de clavecin* (1741).

Other Composers of the Era

*The Italian style and the French style have for long divided
the Republic of Music in France.*

FRANÇOIS COUPERIN (C.1626–61)

The Baroque era produced a plethora of minor composers, many of whom are remembered today only for a handful of works.

Italy

Among these was the Italian priest and singer Gregorio Allegri (1582–1652), who worked at the Sistine Chapel in Rome. His chief claim to fame is the nine-part Miserere which he wrote for the exclusive use of the chapel, and which was jealously guarded until the young prodigy Mozart wrote it out from memory after hearing it twice on a visit in 1770.

Giacomo Carissimi (1605–74), who worked in Rome as choir-master to Queen Christina of Sweden, adapted Monteverdi's operatic style to the sacred oratorio, of which he wrote

ABOVE: Gregorio Allegri (1582–1652), noted particularly for his nine-part Miserere.

over a dozen, together with many motets and cantatas. He was the last composer to use the ancient folk tune "L'homme armé" as the musical basis for a Mass setting.

Carissimi's pupil Alessandro Scarlatti (1660–1725) also worked for Queen Christina, and spent his life moving between Rome and Naples in the service of court and church. More than half of his 115 operas survive, but only a handful, including *La Griselda* (1721), have been revived. Scarlatti invented the *da capo* aria, with its long introduction and closing orchestral *ritornello*. He is credited with introducing recitative accompanied by orchestra rather than keyboard, and invented the "Italian overture", a two-part slow-fast orchestral introduction

to a dramatic work, which later developed into the symphony. He also wrote a large volume of sacred music, and around 700 chamber cantatas.

The Venetian composer Tomaso Albinoni (1671–1751) is now more famous for one work which he did not compose – the Adagio for organ and strings constructed from musical fragments by Remo Giazotto in 1945 – than for his genuine 81 operas, 99 sonatas, 59 concertos and nine sinfonias. His solo concertos for oboe (the earliest known) and trumpet, and some of his *concerti grossi*, are now back in the repertoire.

Giovanni Battista Pergolesi (1710–36) died of tuberculosis at the age of only 26. Many of his works were lost, but he is remembered for a brilliant comic opera, *La serva padrona*

ABOVE: Alessandro Scarlatti (1660–1725), father of Domenico, and a noted composer in his own right.

ABOVE: Giovanni Battista Pergolesi (1710–36), a highly talented composer who died young of tuberculosis.

ABOVE: *An atmospheric contemporary portrait of the great Italian violinist and composer Giuseppe Tartini (1692–1770).*

(*The Maid as Mistress*, 1733), a Stabat Mater (1736), and for tunes he probably did not write (but which were ascribed to him after his death because of his popularity) which Stravinsky recycled in his ballet *Pulcinella* (1920).

Like Corelli, Giuseppe Tartini (1692–1770) is remembered for his daringly original violin music. A brilliant virtuoso, he wrote 42 violin sonatas of immense technical difficulty (the most famous is the *Devil's Trill*, said to have been played to him in a dream by the Devil), 135 violin concertos, and many other instrumental pieces.

France
In France, the vacuum left by Lully's death in 1687 was filled by Marc-Antoine Charpentier (c.1645–1704), who began his career as music master and court singer to the Duchesse de Guise. From 1672 until 1686 he was also associated with Molière's troupe, writing music for the original production of *Le malade imaginaire*, among other works. He wrote a great deal of fine sacred music: 10 Magnificats, 37 antiphons, 84 psalms, over 200 motets and four Te Deums (one of which is now often performed) for Sainte-Chapelle on the Ile de Paris. Among his many fine stage works, *Les arts florissants* (1685–6) has lent its name to one of the foremost modern French ensembles playing music of the Baroque period.

Another French composer, François Couperin (c.1626–61), worked for the courts of Louis XIV and Louis XV. Born into a famous musical dynasty (his uncle Louis was a fine composer for organ and harpsichord), François became organist at the royal chapel. His harpsichord works (four published volumes contain around 230 pieces) are masterpieces of delicacy and musical description; many have enigmatic titles. He also wrote several instrumental suites in the fashionable style of Corelli.

Germany
The composer Johann Hasse (1699–1783) concentrated on opera, becoming director of the Dresden court opera. In 1763 he moved to Vienna, where he continued to write *opere serie* on texts by Metastasio, even though fashions were changing.

ABOVE: *François Couperin, known as "Le grand" ("the Great"), one of the finest composers of keyboard music of his time.*

Georg Philipp Telemann (1681–1767) spent most of his career as music director to the Hamburg churches. Probably the most prolific composer in the history of music (his output includes 600 overtures, 40 operas, 44 Passion settings and a huge quantity of instrumental music), he was in his day more highly regarded than Bach. His instrumental music is still popular today.

ABOVE: *Johann Hasse (1699–1783), upon hearing the 15-year-old Mozart, remarked "This boy will cause us all to be forgotten."*

ABOVE: *Georg Philipp Telemann (1681–1767) holds the record as the most prolific composer of all time.*

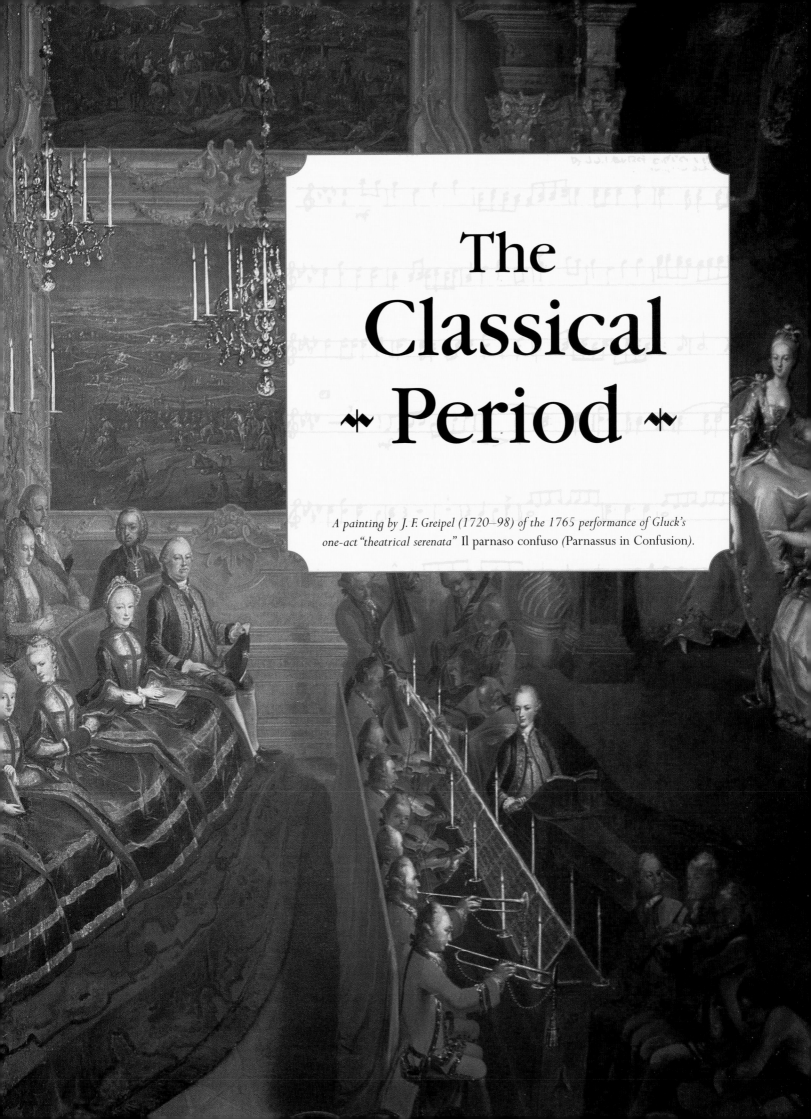

The Classical ✦ Period ✦

A painting by J. F. Greipel (1720–98) of the 1765 performance of Gluck's one-act "theatrical serenata" Il parnaso confuso *(Parnassus in Confusion).*

Music of the Enlightenment

Dust as we are, the immortal spirit grows
Like harmony in music.

WILLIAM WORDSWORTH (1770–1850), "THE PRELUDE"

By classical music, most people today mean serious music of any period, as opposed to jazz, pop, rock or other similar genres. But the term Classical is strictly applied to music written between about 1750–1830, corresponding to a period of classicism in art and architecture.

Classical style

During this period, the flamboyant, heavily ornate Baroque style of architecture (exemplified by the interior of the church of St Nicholas in Prague's Old Town, where Mozart played the organ on one of his visits) gave way to a cooler, more restrained style, based on the serene proportions of the ancient world. The 18th century was the age of the Grand Tour, when upper-class young men were despatched to Italy to study Greek and Roman

ABOVE: The building which inspired much 17th- and 18th-century neo-classical architecture – the Parthenon (Temple of Athena) on the Acropolis in Athens, built between 447 and 422 BC.

architecture, as revealed through recent archaeological excavations.

Contemporary architects such as Robert Adam designed grand country houses with Classical façades, while the furniture designed by Sheraton and his colleagues took on a graceful, delicate look. In England, the fashion for the

ABOVE: A fine example of 18th-century neo-classical architecture – designs for Home House in Portman Square, London, by Robert Adam (1728–92).

ABOVE: Vienna in the 18th century – a view of one of its main streets, the Kohlmarkt. St Michael's Church can be seen on the right.

Classical look reached its height around the turn of the 19th century (the age of Jane Austen), continuing into the Regency period (1811–20). In France, particularly, there was a short period of transition between the Baroque and Classical styles known as Rococo, characterized by delicate but elaborate ornamentation, as seen in French furniture of the mid 18th century, and the paintings of artists such as Antoine Watteau (1684–1721) and François Boucher (1703–70).

Classical style in music

Musical tastes inevitably followed the decorative arts, and the florid, ornamental, technically intricate styles of late Baroque composers gave way to a new emphasis on clarity, order and balance, exemplified by the Classical symphony, string quartet and solo sonata. A few composers fitted the Rococo label, including C. P. E. Bach, François Couperin, the English composer William Boyce (1710–79), and Gluck and Rameau – both primarily opera composers – in some of their works. But generally speaking, the Classical period in musical history is dominated by four giants, all associated with Vienna, and sometimes collectively known as the First Viennese School. They were Haydn, Mozart, Beethoven and Schubert. Their works are still part of the core repertoire of classical music as a whole.

Music's place in society

The late 18th century was a period of great social upheaval. The breakdown of the old social order reached its culmination in the French Revolution (1789–99), and music ceased to be the exclusive preserve of pampered aristocrats or prelates. This radical social shift is reflected in the careers of the four great Classical composers.

Haydn, the oldest, spent his long career in the service of a single

ABOVE: A charming example of 18th-century Rococo art – The Dance *(c.1719) by Antoine Watteau (1684–1721), a favourite artist at the French court.*

aristocratic family, who regarded him as a valued servant. Mozart began his career in a similar way, in the employment of the Archbishop of Salzburg, but when more lucrative court appointments eluded him, he took the radical step of trying a freelance existence, which allowed

ABOVE: Private music-making – The Lost Chord *by Stephen Lewin (fl.1890–1910).*

him personal liberty, but failed to provide sufficient financial security.

Beethoven, in a similar situation, enjoyed the friendship and patronage of several wealthy noblemen, but he was not so fettered by 18th-century convention as Mozart. He understood his own worth as an individual, and his patrons played to his tune, not the other way round. Beethoven was one of the first composers to free himself from the idea of musician as servant, and to produce powerfully individualistic music which he himself promoted to an audience of the rising middle class.

Schubert, a native of Vienna, never tried to obtain a permanent job. A composer who stood on the threshold of the Romantic age, he wrote music out of personal choice, aimed at people like himself (he had a close circle of musically inclined friends). Much of his music – particularly his songs and chamber music – was intended for a domestic market, and none of his symphonies was professionally performed during his lifetime.

Christoph Willibald Gluck

*Hearing "Iphigénie" I forget that I am in an opera house
and think I am hearing a Greek tragedy.*

BARON GRIMM

Gluck's career overlapped with that of Rameau, his senior by over 30 years, and like Rameau, he worked during the transitional period between Baroque and Classical styles, often known as the Rococo age. Born into a German family of foresters who lived in Upper Bohemia, he escaped being coerced into the family profession by running away from home when he was about 13. He went to Prague, and then to Vienna, where he was attached to a nobleman's household. When the nobleman moved to Milan, Gluck went with him, and it was in Italy that he realized his true profession – that of opera composer.

By 1744 eight of his operas had been produced in Italy, many based on

ABOVE: *Christoph Willibald Gluck, painted by Duplessis in 1775, when Gluck was alternating between Vienna and Paris.*

libretti by the great Italian dramatist Pietro Metastasio. In 1745 Gluck went to London, where he found himself in competition with Handel (who is said to have remarked that "Gluck knows no more of counterpoint than my cook", though in fact he liked Gluck and arranged a concert with him). After leaving London, Gluck spent several peripatetic years travelling around Europe with an Italian opera company, before making an advantageous marriage and settling in Vienna. In 1754 the Empress Maria Theresa appointed him composer to the court theatre.

"Reform" operas

Over the next few years Gluck evolved the operatic style which would make him famous. It was clear that *opera seria*, and its French equivalent, the *tragédie-lyrique*, had run their course. Audiences were beginning to demand different types of entertainment, portraying real people in real-life situations rather than cardboard-cutout ancient heroes. To Gluck's mind, opera had been taken over by the often absurd demands of star singers, who felt able to dictate their wishes to librettists and composers, usually in defiance of dramatic reason. In collaboration with the poet Raniero de Calzabigi (1714–95), and with the active encouragement of the Intendant of

ABOVE: *Gluck at the keyboard, by the French artist Eugène Delacroix.*

ABOVE: *The opening of Act II of Gluck's "azione teatrale",* Orfeo ed Euridice.

Life and works

NATIONALITY: German

BORN: Erasbach, 1714;
DIED: Vienna, 1787

SPECIALIST GENRES:
Opera in Italian and French.

MAJOR WORKS: *Orfeo
ed Euridice* (1762); *Alceste*
(1767); *Iphigénie en Aulide*
(1774); *Iphigénie en
Tauride* (1779).

ABOVE: A design by V. D. Polenov (1844–1927) for Act I of Gluck's opera Orfeo ed
Euridice, *for a performance of the French version in Moscow, 1897.*

the court theatres, Count Giacomo Durazzo, Gluck set out to "reform" operatic convention.

He began by writing a series of comic operas in the French style, including *La fausse esclave* and *L'île de Merlin* (1758), but his first major collaboration with Calzabigi and the choreographer Gasparo Angiolini was the ballet *Don Juan* (1761), a work of great dramatic force which influenced Mozart's opera *Don Giovanni* (1787). It was followed in 1762 by the opera *Orfeo ed Euridice* – the most expressive setting of this tragic love story since Monteverdi. Orfeo's aria "Che farò senza Euridice" is one of the most affecting operatic laments, while the scenes in Hades and Elysium (especially the famous "Dance of the Blessed Spirits") gave Gluck ample opportunity for dramatic instrumental and vocal effects, backed up by innovative staging.

In 1767, Gluck and Calzabigi produced the second of their "reform" operas, *Alceste*. In a famous preface to the score, Gluck laid out the principles of this new type of opera, free of the

abuses "which have so long disfigured Italian opera and made of the most splendid and beautiful of spectacles the most ridiculous and wearisome". Gluck aimed to "restrict music to its true

ABOVE: The title page of the first edition of the score of Orfeo ed Euridice, *published in Paris in 1764.*

office of serving the poetry by means of expression and by following the situations of the story", seeking "a beautiful simplicity", free of unnecessary vocal display at the whims of individual singers. He also tried to make the overture an integral part of the drama. These principles governed his next Viennese opera, *Paride ed Elena* (*Paris and Helen*, 1770).

In 1774 Gluck moved to Paris, where over the next six years he wrote three new operas (two based on the story of Iphigenia, and *Echo et Narcisse*), as well as revisions (in French) of *Orfeo* and *Alceste*. He also found himself drawn into competition with the Italian composer Niccolò Piccinni (1728–1800). After *Echo et Narcisse* failed to please, Gluck returned to Vienna, where he died of the last of a series of strokes incurred, it was said, after drinking an after-dinner liqueur in defiance of his doctor's instructions.

Joseph Haydn

So far as genius can exist in a man who is merely virtuous,
Haydn had it.

FRIEDRICH NIETZSCHE (1844–1900)

Joseph Haydn was the eldest and longest lived of the four great composers of the so-called "First Viennese School". Born when Bach and Handel were at the height of their fame, he outlived his friend Mozart by 18 years, and saw his former pupil Beethoven well established in his own career. It was Haydn who practically invented the Classical musical forms of symphony, concerto, string quartet and sonata. Mozart, Beethoven and Schubert all owed an incalculable debt to their genial, hard-working predecessor.

Haydn's life spanned a period of great social change. He was one of the last major musicians to work for a single aristocratic patron – in his case, the Hungarian Esterházy family, whose seat was the castle of Eisenstadt, some 80km (50 miles) from Vienna.

ABOVE: *Joseph Haydn at the keyboard (c.1795) with the score of his penultimate symphony – the* Drumroll *(No. 103).*

The arrangement worked quite well for Haydn – his employers treated him fairly – but in their eyes he was no better than a servant. His life-long desire for freedom was granted only towards the end of his long career, when he was effectively pensioned off and was able to travel and enjoy his spreading European reputation.

Early years

Haydn was one of 12 children born to the village wheelwright in Rohrau, about 50km (30 miles) south-east of Vienna. When he was only six, his budding musical talent was noticed by his family and neighbours, and a relative in Hainburg, who was a schoolmaster, offered to take the child as a boarder and begin his musical education. Shortly after his eighth birthday, Haydn was taken on as a choirboy at St Stephen's

LEFT: *Prince Nikolaus Esterházy ("the Magnificent"), Haydn's patron and employer from 1762–90.*

RIGHT: *The courtyard of the Esterházy family palace at Eisenstadt, near Vienna, where Haydn worked.*

ABOVE: *A performance in 1775 of Haydn's opera* L'incontro improviso (The Unforeseen Encounter), *in the theatre at Eszterháza. The composer is playing the harpsichord.*

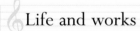

Life and works

NATIONALITY: Austrian

BORN: Rohrau, 1732;
DIED: Vienna, 1809

SPECIALIST GENRES:
Symphonies, string quartets,
opera, oratorios, Masses.

MAJOR WORKS:
15 surviving operas;
104 symphonies; violin and
keyboard concertos;
string quartets; keyboard
sonatas; chamber music
and songs; 12 Masses; Stabat
Mater (1767); *Die Schöpfung*
(1797–8); *Die Jahreszeiten*
(1798–1801).

Cathedral in Vienna, under the harsh regime of the choir-master Karl Georg Reutter. Haydn said later in life: "I never had a proper teacher. I started with the practical side…I listened more than I studied, and tried to turn to good account all the things that impressed me."

Haydn left the choir in 1749, and for the next decade he eked out a meagre living in Vienna as a music teacher. His major breakthrough came when Prince Paul Anton Esterházy happened to hear a symphony of Haydn's and immediately offered the young composer a job. Haydn accepted, but first he took the disastrous step of getting married. His first love had become a nun, and perhaps out of a mistaken sense of duty to her father, Haydn agreed to marry her elder sister, Maria Anna Keller. His wife turned out to be bad-tempered,

unattractive, and didn't care "whether her husband was a cobbler or an artist". She was also apparently unable to have children. During the years ahead Haydn found consolation with other women, but by the time his wife died in 1800 he was too old to think of remarriage.

ABOVE: *The exquisite mirrored concert room at the summer palace of Eszterháza, built in the mid 1760s.*

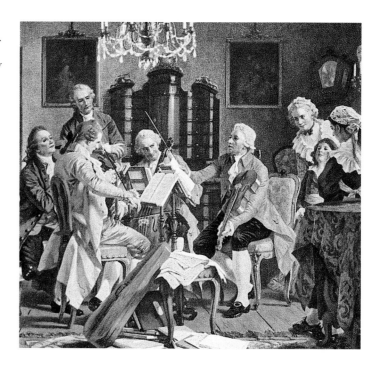

LEFT: A 19th-century edition of Haydn's Symphony No. 84 in E flat, first published as the fourth of the set of six Paris Symphonies.

RIGHT: A 19th-century artist's impression of Haydn and friends playing string quartets. Haydn was a good violinist.

Eisenstadt

In May 1761 Haydn took up his new post. His duties included training the choir and orchestra at Eisenstadt, maintaining all the instruments and music, and keeping discipline. He was also required to compose to order. Among the first works that Haydn wrote for his new patron were three symphonies called *Morning*, *Noon* and *Evening*, possibly intended to be played by the prince himself.

Less than a year later, Prince Paul Anton died. His successor, his brother Prince Nikolaus, was far more socially ambitious (he acquired the nickname "the Magnificent"), and soon Haydn found himself turning out a stream of music for his patron's entertainment: symphonies, concertos, string quartets, trios, and a vast quantity of chamber music for the prince's own instrument, the archaic, six-stringed baryton (similar to the viola d'amore).

Move to Eszterháza

In 1764 Nikolaus decided that Eisenstadt was no longer equal to his pretensions. He ordered the construction of a new summer palace – fit for a prince – on the shores of Lake Neusiedler. It had 126 lavishly decorated guest rooms, an art gallery, a concert hall, a ballroom and a 400-seat theatre. The Empress Maria Theresa attended a performance of one of Haydn's operas there in 1775, and declared: "If I want to hear a good opera, I go to Eszterháza." All in all, Haydn wrote some 25 operas for Eszterháza, including *L'infedeltà delusa* (*Infidelity Deluded*, 1773), *Il mondo della luna* (*The World on the Moon*, 1777) and *Armida* (1783).

While Haydn enjoyed the isolation of Eszterháza, where there was no one to bother him, and he was, as he said, "forced to become original", the other musicians hated it. Each year Prince Nikolaus found it harder to tear himself away from his fairy-tale palace, and he and his courtiers spent as little time at Eisenstadt as possible. But many of the court musicians had families in Vienna, and they begged Haydn to intercede with the prince.

ABOVE: A romantic impression of Haydn walking in the streets of Vienna carrying one of his scores under his arm.

His witty answer was the *Farewell* Symphony (No. 45), written in November 1772, in which one by one the musicians left the stage, packing up their instruments and blowing out their candles, until only two violins were left playing. The prince apparently took the hint.

The *Farewell* Symphony is one of a group of distinctive symphonies written during the 1770s in the fashionable, literary-influenced style known as *Sturm und Drang* ("storm and stress"). Many are in unusual keys, and exhibit a wide variety of moods. The same emotional style also influenced Haydn's other work of the period, including his highly original string quartets – of which he wrote 68 – and piano sonatas.

International fame

By the 1780s, Haydn's international reputation was spreading rapidly, and he managed to negotiate a new contract with his employer which

ABOVE: A romantic impression of Haydn crossing the English Channel in the 1790s.

ABOVE: Haydn's last public appearance, at a performance of his oratorio The Creation *in the Great Hall of the University of Vienna on 27 March 1808, in honour of his 76th birthday.*

allowed him to compose for other patrons, and to have his works published. In 1785 he became a Freemason, and around the same time he was commissioned to write several symphonies by a Parisian masonic lodge. The result was the "Paris" symphonies (Nos. 82–7) – several of which carry nicknames such as *The Bear*, *The Hen* and *The Queen* (a tribute to Marie Antoinette). Their success helped to consolidate his fame abroad.

After the death of Prince Nikolaus Esterházy in 1790, Haydn was free to travel for the first time. He was persuaded by the impresario Johann Peter Salomon to visit London, where he was – to his surprise – fêted by the court and high society. In July 1791 Oxford University honoured him with the degree of Doctor of Music. His twelve "London" symphonies (Nos. 93–104, some again with nicknames including *The Surprise*, *The Miracle*, *The Military* and *The Clock*) met with great public enthusiasm. Haydn made a further trip to England in 1794–5, but resisted King George III's invitation to stay permanently.

Last years

Haydn returned to Vienna as *Kapellmeister* to a new Esterházy prince, Nikolaus II, who in contrast to his predecessors required only sacred music for his newly austere court. Between 1796 and 1802 Haydn produced six fine masses, including the *Missa in tempore belli* (*Mass in Time of War*) and the *Missa in Angustiis* (*Nelson Mass*), both reflecting the political turmoil of the Napoleonic wars. He also wrote two Handelian oratorios, *Die Schöpfung* (*The Creation*, 1798) and *Die Jahreszeiten* (*The Seasons*, 1801). These, his last major works, teem with vibrant detail and an undimmed creative impulse.

The increasingly frail composer made his last public appearance at a performance of *The Creation* at Vienna University in honour of his 76th birthday, and died at the end of May 1809, during the Napoleonic occupation of Vienna. The whole art-loving world of Vienna attended his memorial service, which included a performance of Mozart's Requiem. Eleven years later his remains were reinterred in the chapel at Eisenstadt.

Wolfgang Amadeus Mozart

Mozart is sunshine.

ANTONÍN DVOŘÁK (1841–1904)

The works of Mozart and Beethoven stand at the heart of Western art music. Until the mid 20th century, Beethoven was perhaps the more revered as a heroic figure, battling against personal misfortune to produce his visionary and powerfully original music; while Mozart's music tended to be dismissed as "galant" and superficial. But over the past half-century, the re-evaluation of Mozart, together with the performance and recording of many of his lesser-known works, has revealed a composer of inestimable profundity and infinite variety, whose music has enriched the lives of performers and listeners alike.

ABOVE: Wolfgang Amadeus Mozart, painted nearly three decades after his death by Barbara Krafft.

Family background

The "miracle whom God let be born in Salzburg" made his appearance on 27 January 1756, the last of seven children born to Leopold Mozart and his wife Anna Maria, and one of only two to survive infancy. Leopold Mozart – a talented violinist, and the author of a successful treatise on violin technique – played in the court orchestra of the Archbishop of Salzburg, one of the most powerful prelates in Austria.

Mozart's relationship with his father was central to his life. Leopold Mozart has been vilified as the archetypal domineering father, dragging his prodigiously talented son around the courts of Europe at an early age, not only subjecting him to the rigours of prolonged travel, but forcing him to display his skills on the keyboard to any bored aristocrat who would pay money to listen; then hectoring him when he grew older, trying to obstruct him from leaving a miserable existence in Salzburg for the excitements of Vienna, and interfering in his personal life. In fact, there is no evidence to suggest that Leopold was motivated by anything other than love and solicitude for his son. The Mozart family was

LEFT: Mozart's birthplace on the Getreidegasse in Salzburg, where the family lived from 1747 until 1773.

RIGHT: Mozart's father Leopold (1719–87), painted in 1756 – the year of his son's birth.

ABOVE: Mozart at the age of six in court dress, painted by P. A. Lorenzoni.

Childhood

At the age of four, Wolfgang began to study keyboard and composition with his father. Wolfgang's elder sister Maria Anna (Nannerl) was also a talented pianist, though once she reached adulthood, the conventions of the time obliged her to confine her talents to the domestic sphere. Leopold saw it as his duty to exhibit his exceptional children to the world. When they were six and 11 respectively, he took them to perform before the Elector of Bavaria at Munich, and the Empress Maria Theresa in Vienna.

In 1763 the whole family undertook a trip to Paris and London, where Wolfgang played to both French and English monarchs. By this time he was already composing: four early keyboard sonatas were published in Paris, and he wrote his first symphonies in London. The family arrived back in Salzburg in November 1766. A further trip to Vienna failed to result in a hoped-for opera commission, but on returning home Mozart wrote one anyway, and *La finta semplice* (*The Pretend Simpleton*) was performed at the Archbishop's palace in May 1769.

very close, and their voluminous correspondence is full of protestations of affection. Leopold's only concern was for Wolfgang's well-being and success. He was one of the few people who fully recognized his son's unique gift, and he took every step to prevent it being squandered.

♪ Life and works

NATIONALITY: Austrian

BORN: Salzburg, 1756; **DIED:** Vienna, 1791

SPECIALIST GENRES: Opera, symphonies, piano concertos, string quartets, church music.

MAJOR WORKS: *Le nozze di Figaro* (1786); *Don Giovanni* (1787); *Così fan tutte* (1790); *Die Zauberflöte* (1791); 21 piano concertos; five violin concertos; concertos for clarinet and other wind instruments; 41 symphonies; 24 string quartets and other chamber music; 17 Masses.

ABOVE: A concert given by the young Mozart in the Redoutensaal (ballroom) of the Schönbrunn Palace in Vienna.

ABOVE: *Leopold Mozart and his two talented children, Maria Anna and Wolfgang, 1763.*

ABOVE: *The young Mozart (aged six) being presented by Joseph II to his wife, the Empress Maria Theresa, at Schönbrunn Palace on 13 October 1762.*

Years of travel

In December 1769 Leopold took Wolfgang to Italy for the first time. After visits to Milan, Florence, Rome and Naples, Mozart received his first opera commission. *Mitridate, rè di ponto* was performed at Christmas 1770 at the Milanese court; but although both it and a further opera, *Lucio Silla*, were well received, Mozart's request for a job was turned down.

Back in Salzburg, Mozart settled down reluctantly as *Konzertmeister* to the court orchestra of a new (and less tolerant) Archbishop, and continued to compose. In January 1775 he and his father travelled together for the last time, to Munich, for the performance of Mozart's comic opera, *La finta giardiniera* (*The Pretend Gardener*). Two years later he asked for another period of leave, for an extended trip to Paris. The Archbishop promptly dismissed him, and Leopold, realizing that his own position was now in jeopardy, decided not to go. Mozart set out with his mother as chaperone.

The trip was a disaster. After a prolonged stay in Mannheim, where Wolfgang fell madly in love with a young singer called Aloysia Weber, he was peremptorily ordered by Leopold on to Paris. There he found the sophisticated French capital totally uninterested in an unknown provincial composer, now too old to be

ABOVE: *A romantic artist's impression of Mozart composing, painted around 1880 by Josef Büche.*

interesting as a prodigy. Although the Paris experience did produce some fine works – the *Paris* Symphony (No. 31) and a concerto for flute and harp (both fashionable French instruments) – there was no financial gain and a severe loss, when Mozart's mother died suddenly. Saddened and disillusioned, Mozart returned home.

Idomeneo

For the next 18 months he buried himself in his official court duties, writing sacred music for the Salzburg court, as well as symphonies, serenades, the Sinfonia Concertante for violin and viola (inspired by the French model) and a double piano concerto for himself and Nannerl. Then, in the summer of 1780, he was commissioned to write a new opera for Munich, on the subject of Idomeneus, king of Crete. *Idomeneo* is Mozart's first great opera – the first in which he demonstrated his extraordinary talent for bringing characters to life, allowing them to express real human emotions through the medium of music.

Vienna: early years

After being fêted in Munich, Mozart felt stifled by the petty humiliations of life in Salzburg. In March 1781 he was summoned to Vienna in the Archbishop's retinue, and took advantage of the rising antagonism between himself and his employer to engineer his own dismissal – albeit "with a box on the ear and a kick on the backside".

To Leopold's dismay, Mozart announced his intention of remaining in Vienna, where he would teach, compose, and give concerts. It was a bold idea, but ultimately an unsuccessful one. Austria was at war with the Turkish Empire, money was short, and fashions ephemeral, but for a few years, Mozart's novelty value paid dividends.

During his first year in Vienna he composed a group of three new piano concertos to play at his own subscription concerts, three magnificent wind serenades, and a new opera, *Die Entführung aus dem Serail* (*The Abduction from the Seraglio*), with a German text and spoken dialogue (a type known as a *Singspiel*). Its success

ABOVE: Mozart's first-floor apartment (with bay-window, second from right) in Vienna. He composed The Marriage of Figaro *there.*

was marred only by the laconic remark of the emperor that it seemed to have "too many notes".

Mozart also got married, much against his father's wishes. His bride, Constanze Weber, was the younger

sister of his first love, Aloysia, who had turned him down. Constanze was an amateur singer: Mozart described her as "kind-natured…not ugly, but no beauty either". She has often been accused of ruining her husband's life by her bad housekeeping, but the accusation seems to have been unfounded, and the marriage – which produced two surviving sons (four other children died in infancy) – was very happy. When Leopold Mozart finally visited his son in 1785, he was much impressed with Wolfgang's fine apartment and high standard of living.

Vienna: middle years

For several years Mozart's new career proved successful. He had a busy teaching and concert programme, for which he turned out a string of piano concertos, raising the genre to new heights of virtuosity, passion and expression. Among these may be singled out the Concerto in D minor (K466), a highly emotional work in the *Sturm und Drang* ("storm and stress") style; and its companion in C major (K467), whose exquisite slow movement featured in the 1967 film *Elvira Madigan*.

ABOVE: Mozart's wife Constanze (1763–1842), painted by Hans Hansen in 1802, 11 years after Mozart's death. She remarried in 1809.

ABOVE: The final page from Mozart's own thematic catalogue of his works, which he kept from 1784 until his death. This page shows entries for the operas Die Zauberflöte *and* La clemenza di Tito, *the Clarinet Concerto and a Masonic cantata, finished in November 1791.*

ABOVE: *Stage set for* The Magic Flute, *designed by Simon Quadligo for a performance in Munich on 27 November 1818.*

Mozart's first love, however, was for opera – the genre which could make or break a composer – and in 1785 he began work on a daring new operatic venture, based on Pierre Beaumarchais's notorious French play *La folle journée, ou le mariage de Figaro*, which had been produced the previous year. This attack on aristocratic morals, disguised as a comedy, had already been banned in Vienna. Mozart's literary collaborator was the Italian adventurer, ex-priest and poet Lorenzo Da Ponte (1749–1838), with whom Mozart also worked on two later operas, *Don Giovanni* and *Così fan tutte*.

Le nozze di Figaro (*The Marriage of Figaro*) is one of the great monuments of Western art – a masterpiece of characterization, quicksilver wit and emotional depth. But Vienna failed to appreciate it. By this time, Mozart's arrogance had made him many enemies, including the powerful court composer, Antonio Salieri. Salieri and his friends were intensely jealous of

Mozart's abundant talent, and did all they could to sabotage the opera's production. (Salieri may not literally have poisoned Mozart, as some later claimed, but he certainly stifled his rival's career.) However, the music-lovers of Prague, where Figaro was

ABOVE: *A seduction scene from Mozart's opera* Don Giovanni *(1787).*

produced in 1787, took the opera to their hearts (the city went "Figaro-mad"), and immediately commissioned a new opera, *Don Giovanni*. Mozart's visit to Prague also produced a new symphony (No. 38), known as the *Prague*.

Vienna: last years

The final years of Mozart's brief life were a dismal catalogue of financial worry, constant moves to cheaper apartments, and failing health. He finally achieved his desire of a court appointment, but only as chamber composer, writing dance music for court balls, for a meagre salary. By June 1788 he was writing begging letters to his fellow Freemasons, asking for loans. *Don Giovanni* had been performed with even less success than *Figaro*.

In the summer of 1788, Mozart wrote his last three symphonies, including the *Jupiter* (No. 41), in the space of a few weeks; it is not known

ABOVE: A scene from Act II Scene 3 of the original 1791 production of The Magic Flute *at the Theater auf der Wieden in Vienna.*

if he ever heard them performed. A third opera written with Da Ponte, *Così fan tutte* (literally, "so do all women"), was premièred in the autumn of 1789, but the emperor died shortly afterwards and all theatres were closed. Two trips to Berlin and Frankfurt to give concerts failed to make any money, and by the end of 1790 Mozart was deeply depressed.

In the spring of 1791, he busied himself with dance music and pieces for mechanical organ and glass harmonica, several works for clarinet, including a fine concerto and quintet, and also with the serious and beautiful Piano Concerto in B flat (K595), a work tinged with melancholy. He also began work on another *Singspiel*, written for an actor-manager friend who ran a small suburban theatre. On the surface, *Die Zauberflöte* (*The Magic Flute*) appears to be an amusing pantomime with glorious music attached. But closer inspection reveals that the piece is infused with Masonic symbolism, including thinly disguised versions of Masonic rites and initiation ceremonies. Mozart was taking an

enormous risk, and it has been suggested – probably wrongly – that he paid for his presumption with his life.

While working on *The Magic Flute*, he received two more commissions, one for an *opera seria*, *La clemenza di Tito* (*The Clemency of Titus*), which was produced in Prague in September 1791 and was to be the last major work of this type, and another for a Requiem Mass. The latter was commissioned anonymously, via an emissary dressed in grey, by a Viennese nobleman whose young wife had died. Mozart's own health was failing by this time, and as he worked on the Requiem, he became obsessed by the idea that it would be his own, and that he was being poisoned. In fact he had advanced kidney disease. He died on the morning of 5 December in his wife's arms. Because he left little money, he was given the cheapest possible funeral in an unmarked grave. Few mourners accompanied the cortège. The unfinished Requiem was completed after his death by Franz Süssmayr, one of his pupils.

ABOVE: A 19th-century artist's impression of Mozart's last hours, by Henry O'Neil (1817–80). The composer died in his wife's arms, aged 35.

Ludwig van Beethoven

Nature would burst should she attempt to produce nothing save Beethovens.

ROBERT SCHUMANN (1810–56)

Mozart died in Vienna in the late autumn of 1791, a victim of the stifling class conventions of the *ancien régime*. A year later, a 20-year-old named Ludwig van Beethoven arrived in Vienna, keen to make his name as a musician. By this time, the face of European society was changing fast. The French Revolution was in full swing, and Austria – horrified at the treatment meted out to the French monarchs, particularly Queen Marie Antoinette, a former Austrian archduchess – had declared war on France. For more than two decades, Europe would be ripped apart by war. While Mozart's life had remained largely unaffected by international politics, Beethoven's revolutionary artistic vision was shaped by the ideology and volcanic social change of the turbulent times in which he lived.

ABOVE: Ludwig van Beethoven (1770–1827), painted in 1823 by Ferdinand Georg Waldmüller.

Early years

Beethoven was born into a musical family. His grandfather had been music director to the Archbishop-Elector of Cologne, and his father was also employed at the electoral court, though in the lowlier position of singer and instrumentalist. As with the Mozart family, the majority of the seven children born to Johann van Beethoven and his wife died in infancy. Three boys survived: Ludwig, born on 16 or 17 December 1770, and two younger brothers, Caspar Carl and Nikolaus.

Johann van Beethoven, an alcoholic bully, was determined that his eldest son should follow in the young Mozart's footsteps as a child prodigy. But Johann lacked Leopold Mozart's abilities as a teacher, and forced his son to practise the keyboard constantly at the expense of his general education. From around 1780 Beethoven received more kindly and sympathetic instruction from the court composer and organist Christian Neefe, who organized the publication of his pupil's first compositions – a set of keyboard variations. In 1783 a set of three piano sonatas appeared in print with a dedication to the elector, whose successor appointed Beethoven second court organist the following year.

In 1787 Neefe suggested that Beethoven should travel to Vienna to take lessons from Mozart, who was much impressed with the young man's talent. But Beethoven's trip was curtailed by news of his mother's serious illness: she died of tuberculosis in the summer of that year, leaving him to cope with his father's violence and alcoholism. At the age of 18 Beethoven assumed responsibility for the family affairs, being granted half his father's court salary as well as his own. He also found an influential patron, Count Ferdinand Waldstein, who persuaded the elector to allow Beethoven leave to study with Haydn in Vienna. The

ABOVE: Beethoven's birthplace in Bonn. He was born in the third-floor attic.

elector agreed, and in 1792 Beethoven
arrived in Vienna, the city which
became his permanent home.

Vienna

Beethoven found that his lessons with
Haydn were not a great success, but
he quickly began to make a name as a
pianist, with a formidable reputation
for improvisation. "He is greatly
admired for the velocity of his playing,
and astounds everybody by the way he
can master the greatest difficulties with
ease," a local paper reported. He also
found a new and powerful patron,
Prince Lichnowsky (in whose mansion

he had an apartment), and despite
his unprepossessing appearance –
stocky, swarthy, with an ugly, red,
pockmarked face – and rather boorish
manners, he found himself tolerated
by fashionable society.

He gave his first public concert,
playing a new piano concerto of his
own, at the Burgtheater on 29 March
1795, astonishing the audience with his
fiery virtuosity and establishing a
pattern which would continue for
several years. By 1796 he had
published a set of piano trios and three
piano sonatas (a genre he would
develop far beyond the Classical
"galant" style of Mozart and Haydn),
and had earned enough money to set
himself up in his own apartment.
Over the next four years he went
on occasional concert tours, gave
subscription concerts in Vienna, and
issued his chamber works in print –
sonatas for piano (including the
magnificent *Pathétique* Sonata No. 8 in
C minor), violin and cello, and the
Op. 16 Quintet for piano and wind.

All these works show Beethoven's
desire to push at the boundaries of
conventional compositional technique,
to expand sonata form, and to infuse
his work with unheard-of drama
and passion.

These principles were already
evident in the first of his nine
symphonies (written in 1800), which,
while conforming to the standard
Classical four-movement format,
relies not so much on lyrical themes
as on rhythmic dynamism and the
development of short melodic
fragments, or motifs. Clearly, the
old courtly "minuet and trio" which
traditionally constituted the third
movement of a symphony had outlived
its purpose: from the Second
Symphony onwards Beethoven
replaced it with a faster, more dynamic
and rhythmically propelled scherzo,
while retaining a tripartite structure
with a slower, more lyrical central
section. "There is something
revolutionary about that music,"
remarked the emperor.

*ABOVE: Beethoven, aged 17, playing to Mozart. Mozart declared that the young genius would
"soon astonish the world".*

ABOVE: A view of rural Heiligenstadt, where Beethoven escaped from city life to compose and recuperate, and where he wrote the "Heiligenstadt Testament".

The Heiligenstadt crisis

Around the turn of Beethoven's 30th year, just as his career seemed to be soaring, he was struck by an appalling personal crisis. He was forced to acknowledge the fact that he was going deaf. For several years he had tried to hide his hearing problems for both professional and social reasons, but it became clear that the affliction was incurable.

In the summer of 1802 he reached a nadir of despair, while staying at the country retreat of Heiligenstadt, just outside Vienna. He wrote a long letter (known as the "Heiligenstadt Testament") to his brothers, in which he described his utter misery: "For me there can be no pleasure in human society, no intelligent conversation, no mutual confidences. I must live like an outcast." But though he had contemplated suicide, Beethoven concluded that he must henceforth live for his art: "It seemed impossible to leave the world before I had accomplished all I was destined to do." The letter was never sent, and was found among his effects after his death.

Years of struggle

Beethoven's inner struggle is reflected in the titanic works of the next few years. These included the massive *Eroica* Symphony (No. 3), originally dedicated to Napoleon, nearly twice as long as a conventional symphony, with a powerful and tragic funeral march as its slow movement; the Triple Concerto for piano, violin and cello; two piano sonatas (No. 21, the *Waldstein* and No. 23, the *Appassionata*); and his only opera, *Fidelio*.

The opera's plot was based on a French Revolutionary tale of a wife's heroic efforts to save her imprisoned husband. (For political reasons, Beethoven was obliged to move the action to 18th-century Spain.) By the time of the opera's production, in 1805, Napoleon's army had occupied Vienna and *Fidelio* received only two performances. It remains a lone masterpiece of its kind in Beethoven's output, perhaps lacking the innate sense of theatre of Mozart's mature operas, but containing memorable dramatic moments such as Leonora's great "Abscheulicher" aria, the quartet "Mir ist so wunderbar" and the moving chorus when the prisoners are brought from their cells and greet the light of day.

ABOVE: The "Heiligenstadt Testament", a letter written in 1802, in which Beethoven expressed his suicidal despair at his deafness.

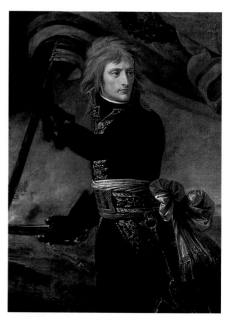

ABOVE: Napoleon Bonaparte (1769– 1821), the original dedicatee of Beethoven's Symphony No. 3 (the Eroica*), but whom Beethoven despised when he proclaimed himself Emperor of France.*

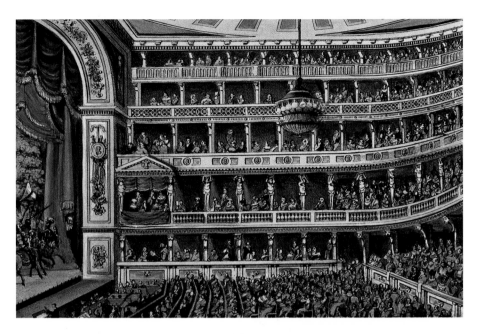

ABOVE: The première of Beethoven's opera Fidelio *at the Theater an der Wien in Vienna, 1805. The opera was not an immediate success, owing to the French occupation.*

Disillusioned after *Fidelio*'s failure, Beethoven concentrated on instrumental pieces, producing a set of three string quartets dedicated to the Russian ambassador to Austria, Count Andreas Razumovsky, the Fourth Symphony, the Violin Concerto (again a lone masterpiece), and his Fourth Piano Concerto. Just before Christmas 1808 the Fifth and Sixth Symphonies, both revolutionary in concept, were premièred at the same concert. The Fifth, with its progression from tragedy to hope, has been interpreted as representing Beethoven's own struggle against adversity, and is one of the first symphonic works to recycle thematic material between movements. The Sixth (the *Pastoral*) is a harbinger of Romanticism. One of the earliest symphonic examples of "tone-painting", it illustrates scenes of Austrian country life, including a realistic thunderstorm, birdsong and a village festival.

By this time, Beethoven was enjoying a measure of financial security through the support of several wealthy patrons, including the Archduke Rudolph (to whom Beethoven dedicated his Fifth Piano Concerto, known as *The Emperor*). When Napoleon's troops invaded Vienna in 1809, the imperial family fled to safety: Beethoven celebrated their return from exile in 1810 with the Piano Sonata No. 26, *Das Lebewohl* (*The Farewell*). Seven years later Rudolph also received the dedication of the *Hammerklavier* Sonata (No. 29).

Disappointment in love

Apart from his deafness, Beethoven's life was marred by his failure to find a partner: the objects of his affection were usually either married, or else above him in social station (such as Countess Giulietta Guicciardi, the dedicatee of the *Moonlight* Sonata). An unsent letter written in 1812 reveals a deep attachment to an unspecified

ABOVE: The triumphant entrance of Napoleon's army into Vienna in 1805. The French occupation caused hardship for Viennese citizens.

ABOVE: Countess Giulietta Guicciardi, to whom the Moonlight *Sonata was dedicated.*

woman, "the immortal beloved", who may possibly have been Antonie Brentano, the wife of a Frankfurt businessman. She and Beethoven never met in later life, but many years later he dedicated to her his last work for piano, the *Diabelli Variations*.

Beethoven seems to have despised women of a lower social class: an attitude which led to acrimonious rows with his brothers over their "unsuitable" choice of wives. In 1820, after a long legal battle begun after his brother's death in 1815, he became sole guardian of his nephew Karl, perhaps fulfilling his own frustrated desire for an heir. Their relationship, however, proved a stormy one, and overshadowed the later years of Beethoven's life.

Last years

In 1813 Beethoven celebrated Napoleon's defeat on the Iberian Peninsula with his *Battle Symphony*. Originally written for a mechanical instrument called the "panharmonicon", the piece is far inferior to the contemporary Seventh and Eighth

ABOVE: A 19th-century artist's impression of Beethoven (in later life) composing in his Viennese apartment. He was notably untidy.

ABOVE: Beethoven's ear-trumpet lying on the manuscript of his Eroica Symphony.

ABOVE: The opening of the Theater in der Josefstadt in Vienna, 1822, for which Beethoven wrote the overture The Consecration of the House.

ABOVE: *The Kärntnertor Theatre in Vienna, where the première of Beethoven's Ninth Symphony took place on 7 May 1824.*

Symphonies. By this time Beethoven had more or less abandoned public performance, and by 1818 he was stone deaf.

He became increasingly withdrawn and anti-social, but continued to compose. Sacred music had never figured largely in his output, but in 1822 he completed the *Missa solemnis*, originally intended to celebrate Archduke Rudolph's enthronement as Archbishop of Olmütz. This great work, written "from the heart to the heart", ranks with Bach's B minor Mass as one of the crowning achievements of its composer's career. Sections of it were performed in May 1824 at a concert which included the première of the Ninth Symphony, the result of Beethoven's desire to write a "choral symphony with voices". Within a traditional symphonic framework (except that the scherzo is placed second), Beethoven burst the bonds of convention by introducing into the finale a setting for solo voices and chorus of Schiller's *An die Freude* (*Ode to Joy*), with its ecstatic vision of an international brotherhood of man.

Beethoven's last instrumental compositions – the last three piano sonatas and the late string quartets (including the six-movement Op. 130, with its immense fugal finale) – have always been regarded as embodying Western musical art at a peak of perfection. They are introspective works, not intended to be "understood" or applauded in the conventional sense. They are the work of a man who had withdrawn into an inner life, which could only be expressed through the medium of pure, abstract music.

In 1826 Beethoven's nephew Karl attempted suicide. By this time the composer (a heavy drinker) was already mortally ill with liver disease. After months of suffering, Beethoven died on 26 March 1827. In contrast to Mozart's low-key burial, 10,000 people are estimated to have watched Beethoven's funeral procession. The poet Franz Grillparzer delivered the funeral oration, in honour of "the man who inherited and enriched the immortal fame of Handel and Bach, of Haydn and Mozart... Until his death he preserved a father's heart for mankind. Thus he was, thus he died, thus he will live to the end of time."

ABOVE: *A contemporary watercolour of Beethoven's funeral procession leaving the "House of the Black Spaniard", his last residence (to the right of the church).*

Franz Schubert

If you go to see him during the day, he says "Hello, how are you? — Good!"
and goes on working, whereupon you go away.

FRANZ VON SCHOBER (1798–1882)

On 29 March 1827, Beethoven was buried in the village cemetery of Währing, just outside Vienna. Among the torch-bearers in the funeral procession was a dark-haired, bespectacled young man of 30. His name was Franz Schubert, and he was paying homage to the member of his own profession he most revered. Less than two years later, Schubert's own body would be interred in the same cemetery, close to Beethoven's grave.

Unlike Beethoven, whose fame during his lifetime had spread all over Europe, Schubert's reputation was largely local. His composing career was short – a mere 15 years – and although he worked in the same genres as his three great predecessors, it was not his operas, or even his symphonies, but his more intimate works, particularly the songs and chamber music, which posthumously ensured his unique place in musical history.

By the time war in Europe ended with the Congress of Vienna (1815), European society had changed dramatically. A new generation of middle-class, independently minded citizens had sprung up, but conservative politicians, such as Prince Metternich in Vienna, attempted to maintain the status quo of the ruling classes and banish "subversive and revolutionary tendencies" by keeping the populace firmly under control through censorship and political repression.

ABOVE: Franz Schubert (1797–1828), aged about 28, painted by Wilhelm August Rieder around 1825.

People sought relief through social activity. Balls and parties became fashionable for the rich, while the less well-off built up a network of like-minded friends, meeting in private homes or at the local coffee houses. This was Schubert's social milieu.

Youth

Vienna was the centre of Schubert's universe. He was born on 31 January 1797 to a suburban schoolmaster, who taught all his children to play musical instruments. Franz learned the viola, and together with his father and brothers made up a string quartet. In 1808 he won a scholarship to the imperial seminary, where he had daily music lessons and played in the school orchestra. He also made several formative friendships, one with Joseph von Spaun, an ex-pupil and law student. By the time Schubert left school at the age of 16, he had already written a substantial quantity of music.

Schubert and Goethe

After his mother's death and his father's remarriage, Schubert spent some time as a teacher at his father's school. He also fell in love with a young singer named Therese

ABOVE: The great writer Johann Wolfgang von Goethe (1749–1832), the father of German Romanticism, painted c.1790.

Grob, who performed in his F major Mass in the autumn of 1814. Perhaps as a result of unrequited love, he began composing songs. His first efforts marked the beginning of a lifelong involvement with the poetry of Europe's most celebrated writer and the "father" of Romanticism, Johann Wolfgang von Goethe (1749–1832). Among these early songs was "Gretchen am Spinnrade" ("Gretchen at the Spinning Wheel"), from Goethe's *Faust*, a masterly characterization of the abandoned Margaret's distress.

The next year produced a huge crop of some 150 songs, many of them settings of Goethe's texts, such as the delicate ballad "Heidenröslein" ("Briar-rose"), and the stormy "Erlkönig" ("The Elf-king"), depicting a father's wild ride through the night to save his sick child from the grasp of Death. In spring 1816 Schubert's friend Spaun sent 28 Goethe settings to the poet, asking permission to dedicate them to him. Goethe, who loathed musical settings of his work, returned the volume without comment. Fortunately undeterred, Schubert went on to add another 100 songs – including the immortal settings of Goethe's "Nur wer die Sehnsucht kennt" ("Only he who knows yearning") and "Kennst du das Land" ("Do you know the country where lemon trees blossom?") – to his canon before the end of the year. In his 20th year he completed his Fourth and Fifth Symphonies, both very much in the Classical mould, for private performance by amateur orchestras.

Maturity

Schubert finally left the family home in December 1816, at the prompting of another close friend, Franz von Schober. A wealthy law student, Schober persuaded Schubert to abandon the drudgery of teaching and concentrate on composition (the song "An die Musik" – "To Music" – is a setting

ABOVE: *The autograph manuscript of Schubert's setting of Goethe's poem "Heidenröslein" ("Briar-rose"), one of his best-known early songs.*

Life and works

NATIONALITY: Austrian

BORN: Vienna, 1797;
DIED: Vienna, 1828

SPECIALIST GENRES: Songs, piano music, symphonies, chamber music.

MAJOR WORKS: Symphonies No. 8 (*Unfinished*, 1822) and No. 9 (*The Great*, 1828); String Quintet in C (1828); Piano Quintet in A (*The Trout*, 1819); Octet in F (1824); String Quartet No. 14 in D minor (*Death and the Maiden*, 1824); Fantasy in C major for piano (*The Wanderer*, 1822); Fantasy in F minor for piano duet (1828); over 600 songs; song-cycles *Die schöne Müllerin* (1823) and *Winterreise* (1827).

of a Schober poem). He also introduced Schubert to the singer Johann Michael Vogl, who became the leading interpreter of his songs. These continued to pour out throughout 1817, together with seven piano sonatas, heavily influenced by Beethoven.

ABOVE: *A view of a Viennese square in Schubert's time. Schubert spent all of his short life in Vienna.*

ABOVE: *An idealized portrait of the composer on his balcony, painted in 1917.*

In 1818 Schubert's Sixth Symphony – a substantial work which shows Beethoven's influence – was performed (again by an amateur orchestra), and he spent five happy months on a Hungarian aristocratic estate as music teacher to the daughters of Count Esterházy of Galanta, concentrating on piano music for his young pupils. "I live and compose like a god", he told a friend.

Life in Vienna

The change of scene encouraged Schubert to broaden his horizons, and the next summer he and Vogl took a holiday in Steyr, where Schubert completed another piano sonata and the *Trout* Quintet, based on his own song "Die Forelle". From then onwards, Schubert's life took a regular shape. In Vienna, he was the focus of a close-knit group of talented young people – writers, poets and students – who enjoyed a happy and carefree existence, meeting at cafés, at parties in each other's homes or, in the summer, at a country estate owned by Schober's uncle. These informal gatherings, with games of charades, poetry readings and performances of Schubert's music, became known as "Schubertiaden". In the summers, Schubert and Vogl went on long walking tours of Upper Austria, where Schubert drew inspiration from the dramatic landscape.

The early 1820s brought mixed fortune. Vogl's performance of "Der Erlkönig" at a concert in the Burgtheater in 1821 brought public recognition for the as yet unpublished composer, but he had no experience of

ABOVE: *Schubert playing the piano during an evening at Joseph von Spaun's.*

business matters, and when demand for his work rose, he rashly sold the copyrights of ten volumes of songs to the publisher Diabelli. And by 1823 it was clear that Schubert's operatic ambitions would never be realized. Of his 17 stage works, none achieved success, and only the charming and popular incidental music to *Rosamunde* has survived.

Tragedy

The same year – 1823 – brought disaster. Schubert's hedonistic existence had left him suffering from syphilis, then a potentially fatal disease. At the height of his illness, he composed the two-movement *Unfinished* Symphony, restless and tragic in mood, as well as the great *Wanderer* Fantasy and the A minor Sonata, both for piano. He also composed his first song-cycle, a new genre consisting of a set of thematically linked songs based on a sequence of poems, telling a story. *Die schöne Müllerin* (*The Fair Maid of the Mill*) is a quintessentially Romantic tale of rejected love and death by drowning.

The last four years of Schubert's life were a constant struggle against

ABOVE: *An excursion of the "Schubertians" from Atzenbrugg to Aumuhl, painted by Schubert's friend Leopold Kupelwieser. Schubert (wearing a top-hat) is walking behind the carriage.*

ABOVE: A "Schubertiad" (Schubert evening) in a Viennese salon. Schubert at the piano is accompanying the singer Johann Michael Vogl.

depression and illness, interspersed with frantic creative activity. As well as the Ninth Symphony (a work of Beethovenian proportions and unstoppable rhythmic impulse, which a Viennese orchestra declared "unplayable"), the works of these years included a great deal of chamber music: the Octet for wind and strings, string quartets in A minor and D minor (Death and the Maiden), two massive piano trios, and the three last piano sonatas (which Schumann memorably described as "purely and simply thunderstorms breaking forth with Romantic rainbows over slumbering worlds").

Last months

Schubert continued to compose songs until the end of his life. Some, such as the radiant "Ständchen" ("Serenade"),

express a passionate delight in life; others – such as the bleak song-cycle Winterreise (Winter Journey), based on

ABOVE: Schubert's spectacles lying on the manuscripts of some of his last works.

poems by Wilhelm Müller – plumb the depths of despair. Among the last was "Der Doppelgänger" – a terrifying setting of a poem by Heinrich Heine in which a young man sees his "double", foretelling his own death. It was a prophetic vision.

By September 1828, Schubert's health had worsened, and he moved in with his brother. That month he completed the sublime String Quintet in C major, followed in October by his last major work, Der Hirt auf dem Felsen (The Shepherd on the Rock), for soprano and piano with clarinet obbligato. He died of typhus on 19 November, aged 31, leaving only an unsurpassed musical legacy. His tombstone in the Währing cemetery carries the telling epitaph by Grillparzer: "The art of music has buried here a rich possession, but still fairer hopes."

Other Composers of the Era

Classicism is health, romanticism is sickness.

Johann Wolfgang von Goethe (1749–1832)

Two sons of J. S. Bach bridged the gap between the Baroque and the Classical eras. Carl Philipp Emmanuel Bach (1714–88), born in Weimar, decided to follow a musical career, and in 1738 became keyboard player to the future Frederick the Great of Prussia. He remained in Berlin until 1767, when he succeeded Telemann as director of music at Hamburg. He is chiefly remembered for his inventive keyboard sonatas (of which he wrote over 200, for both "connoisseurs and amateurs"), which played a major role in the development of sonata form. His sinfonias, concertos and flute sonatas are also still performed today.

C. P. E. Bach taught the harpsichord to his younger brother Johann Christian Bach (1735–82). Bach's

ABOVE: Thomas Augustine Arne (1710–78), the composer of "Rule, Britannia!"

youngest son continued his studies in Italy, where he began a career as an opera composer, but moved to London in 1762 and remained there until his death, becoming known as "the English Bach". He was initially composer to the King's Theatre in London, and was later appointed music master to Queen Charlotte. His later operas were not very successful, but his instrumental works – particularly his skilfully crafted sinfonias and 40 or so piano concertos – had great influence on Haydn, Beethoven, and particularly Mozart, who met Bach when he visited London at the age of eight.

While British music in the 18th century was largely dominated by European imports, Thomas Arne (1710–78) was a notable home-grown

exception. Arne's output was largely theatrical, including masques and operas (his 1740 masque *Alfred* contained the song "Rule, Britannia!"), but he also wrote some charming symphonies, keyboard concertos and sonatas, and songs, including "The British Grenadiers".

Muzio Clementi (1752–1832) was born in Rome, but lived mostly in England. A brilliant pianist, who later went into publishing and piano-making, he toured Europe as a virtuoso from 1781–83, but then settled in London, where he became a much sought-after teacher (his pupils included John Field). Clementi's own compositions, which include sonatas, sonatinas and studies for piano, are still used as teaching pieces.

ABOVE: Carl Philipp Emmanuel Bach (1714–88), J. S. Bach's third son, who was an influential composer.

ABOVE: J. S. Bach's youngest son, Johann Christian Bach (1735–82), "the English Bach", who worked mostly in London.

ABOVE: *Luigi Boccherini (1743–1805), who worked in Vienna and Madrid. He was a fine cellist.*

Muzio Clementi's German contemporary, Johann Nepomuk Hummel (1778–1837), studied the piano with Mozart, and also worked for Haydn's employer Prince Esterházy. From 1819–37 he was

ABOVE: *The Italian Domenico Cimarosa (1749–1801), court composer in St Petersburg and Vienna, playing the clavichord.*

Kapellmeister to the Weimar court. His fluent, tuneful works were very popular: his Trumpet Concerto (1803) is still much performed, as are his *Septet militaire* (1829) and a Piano Quintet of 1802. His piano concertos and sonatas influenced Chopin.

While the Classical period was dominated by the four Viennese giants, Italy continued to produce its fair share of talented composers. Among them was Luigi Boccherini (1743–1805), whose music is similar in style to Haydn's. He worked in Vienna from 1757–64, but in 1769 moved to Madrid as composer to the Spanish court. An enormously prolific composer, Boccherini left a vast output of chamber music, including 91 string quartets, 154 quintets and 60 trios, as well as symphonies, concertos and church music. His famous Minuet (featured in the 1955 British film *The Ladykillers*) comes from his String Quintet in E, Op. 13, No. 5.

Mozart's rival Antonio Salieri (1750–1825) worked principally in Vienna, where he was first an opera composer, and then court conductor. His operas, unlike Mozart's, have not survived, but he was an influential teacher; Beethoven, Schubert and Liszt were among his pupils.

Domenico Cimarosa (1749–1801) spent some time in St Petersburg as court composer to Catherine the Great of Russia, before succeeding Salieri as court *Kapellmeister* in Vienna. After 1792 he returned to his native Naples. Most of his 65 operas have been forgotten, with the single exception of the comic opera *Il matrimonio segreto* (*The Secret Marriage*, 1792). He also wrote an oboe concerto, around 30 keyboard sonatas, and other instrumental works.

His rival and contemporary Giovanni Paisiello (1740–1816) also worked in St Petersburg and Naples, producing

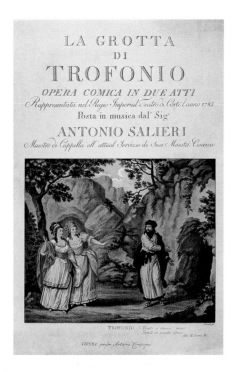

ABOVE: *The title page of a comic opera by Antonio Salieri, produced a few months after Mozart's* Marriage of Figaro, *in 1785.*

over 100 operas as well as symphonies and piano concertos. His 1782 opera *Il barbiere di Siviglia* (*The Barber of Seville*), written when he was court composer to Catherine the Great, was at first more popular than Rossini's later version.

ABOVE: *Giovanni Paisiello (1740–1816), one of the most successful opera composers of his time, painted by Elisabeth Vigée-Lebrun.*

Glossary

Ars antiqua: (old art) style of medieval music based on plainsong and organum.

Ars nova: (new art) musical style of 14th-century France and Italy, less restrictive than *ars antiqua*, introducing new rhythms and more independent parts.

Basso continuo: ("figured bass") an accompanying bass line for a keyboard instrument, with figures to indicate chords on which the player improvises.

Canon: a composition in which a melody begun in one part is repeated in another part, or parts, before the first has finished.

Cantata: an extended choral work (sometimes with solo parts), usually with orchestral accompaniment.

Clef: the sign that fixes the position of a particular note on the staff.

Coda: extra section at the end of a movement.

Concerto: a work for solo instrument(s) and orchestra, usually in three movements.

Concerto grosso: instrumental form contrasting a small group of instruments with a larger orchestral group.

Consort: a group of instruments, such as viols.

Counterpoint: the weaving together of two or more melodic lines to make musical sense, resulting in polyphony.

Development: in sonata form, the section of a movement following the initial statement of the themes, in which they are expanded or modified.

Exposition: the first part of sonata form, in which the main themes are stated.

Fugue: contrapuntal work in three or more parts of equal importance, which enter successively in imitation of each other.

Ground bass: a short bass theme persistently repeated.

Harmony: the simultaneous sounding of different notes.

Homophony: music in which the parts move together, presenting a top melody with chords beneath.

Isorhythmic: Of motets, having a tenor line in which the rhythm, though not the pitch, is repeated many times.

Key: the classification of the notes of a scale, determined by the key-note.

Minuet: French rustic dance in triple time adapted to court use in the 17th century, and to symphonic use in the 18th century.

Mode: name for each of the ways of ordering the notes of a scale.

Motet: Ecclesiastical vocal musical form based on a given melody with other parts in counterpoint.

Motif, motive: a recognizable short group of notes.

Neume: a sign in medieval notation showing the pitch of a syllable of vocal music.

Oratorio: an extended musical setting of a religious text in semi-dramatic form.

Overture: (1) an orchestral opening movement to an opera, play or suite; (2) an orchestral work in one movement, usually with a title alluding to a literary or pictorial source.

Plainsong: medieval church music consisting of a single line of unaccompanied music sung in "free" rhythm.

Polyphony: the simultaneous sounding of different melodic lines, in counterpoint.

Prelude: a musical introduction, or a short self-contained piece.

Recapitulation: in sonata form, the section of a movement which repeats the original themes after the development.

Recitative: speech-like singing in opera used for dialogue or to precede an aria.

Scherzo: (a joke) a lively movement in a symphony developed by Beethoven to replace the minuet and trio.

Sonata: an instrumental work in three or four movements and for one or two players.

Sonata form: a construction used in the first movement of a sonata or symphony, which is divided into three sections: exposition, development and recapitulation.

Song-cycle: a set of songs grouped by the composer in a particular order for performance, often based on a sequence of poems.

Suite: an instrumental piece in several movements.

Symphony: a substantial orchestral work, usually in four movements.

Tenor: the highest normal male voice, so called because it held the melody in plainsong.

Tonality: the general key of a piece.

Trio: (1) a combination of three performers; (2) a work for three performers; (3) the centre section of a minuet, traditionally written in three parts.

Index

...ledgements

has been ... made
ge the pictures
owever, we apologize
any unintentional
is, which will be corrected
re editions.

AKG, London: 1; 3; 6r; 7tr; 8–9;
15t; 20t, bl; 22b; 28t; 38b; 40t;
44t; 45t; 46t; 48t; 50t; 53t; 54t,
bl, br; 56t, bl, br; 57t, b; 58b; 59tl;
62t; 63t; 64bl; 68t; 70br; 71b;
72t; 73t; 75b; 76t, bl; 78tl, tr, b;
79bl; 80t; 81t; 82t, b; 84bl; 86t;
88t; 92bl, br; *British Library* 10r;
Stefan Diller 23t; *Erich Lessing* 30b;
38t; 51b; 66–7; 68br; 69t; 75t;
77t; 79t; 85t; 86bl, br; 87b; 91b;
Visioars 84br.
Arena Images Ltd: *Ron Scherl*
39t.
Art Archive Ltd: 15b; 35t; 52b;
84t.

**Bridgeman Art Library,
London:** 4; 5; 14; 18–19; 21b;
25t, b; 26t, b; 31b; 33b; 36–7;
39t, b; 40b; 46bl; 47b; 48b; 49tr,
b; 60t; 61bl, br; 65tl, br; 68bl;
69b; 77b; 81b; 85bl; 89b; 90b;
91t; 93tl, br; *Giraudon* 47b; 88b;
David Lees 40b.

gettyone Stone: 43t.
Lebrecht Collection, London:
2; 10l; 11tr, b; 12; 13l, r; 16–17;
20br; 21t; 24t, bl, br; 27t, b; 28b;
29t, b; 30t; 31t; 32t, b; 33t; 34t, b;
35bl, br; 41bl, br; 42t; 43b; 44br;
45b; 46br; 47t; 49tl; 50br; 51t;
52t; 53b; 55b; 58t; 59tr; 60bl, br;
64t, br; 65tr, bl; 70t, bl; 71t; 72bl;
74tl, tr, b; 76br; 83; 85br; 87t; 89t;
90tl, tr; *M. Allen* 42b; 54tr; 93tr, bl;
Joanne Harris 61t; *R. Meek* 22t;
Private Collection 63b; 80b; *Celene
Rosen* 11tl; 50bl; *Royal Academy of
Music* 62b; 92t; *G. Salter* 72br; 73b.
Performing Arts Library: *Fritz
Curzon* 15br.
Wendy Thompson: 23b; 55tl;
British Library 79br; *Editions des
Musées Nationaux* 44bl.